The Pearson Lab Manual for Developing Writers
Volume B: Paragraphs

Linda Copeland

St. Louis Community College, Meramec

Longman

New York   Boston   San Francisco

London   Toronto   Sydney   Tokyo   Singapore   Madrid

Mexico City   Munich   Paris   Cape Town   Hong Kong   Montreal

The Pearson Lab Manual for Developing Writers: Volume B: Paragraphs

Copyright © 2010 Pearson Education, Inc.

17— EBM —14 13

Longman
is an imprint of

www.pearsonhighered.com

ISBN 10:   0 -205-69341-5

ISBN 13: 978-0-205-69341-2

Preface

The Pearson Lab Manual for Developing Writers series has been designed as supplements for any developmental writing text organized along the rhetorical modes. The paragraph and essay workbook exercises illustrate key concepts and encourage students to apply these concepts, which are covered in most writing classes, i.e., audience, topic sentences, thesis statements, coherence, unity, and levels of development. The analysis exercises isolate concepts explained in class and in the primary text and allow students to demonstrate their understanding of these concepts. The building exercises allow students to apply the concepts and provide students with the "raw materials" to develop paragraphs and essays.

For many developmental students, the biggest hurdle to writing is simply coming up with something to say. Some of the paragraph and essay exercises provide much of the information, allowing the students to focus on articulating the main idea and developing organizing strategies. Other writing prompts encourage the students to develop their own ideas through guided prewriting exercises. The revision prompts direct the students' attention to specific key elements of their own writing and to assess whether they have met the needs of their reading audience. Throughout the paragraph and essay workbooks, audience and purpose stay at the forefront of the writing exercises.

The sentence skills workbook provides exercises that apply grammar, punctuation and mechanics rules rather than simply offer skills drills. Composing exercises that highlight specific sentence skills explained in the students' primary text make up most of the exercises. Even those exercises that require students to simply insert a punctuation mark or to choose between two words go further in requiring the student to provide the rationale behind the choices.

What all of the workbooks have in common is that they are built around topics that draw from history, science, popular culture and other areas that not only engage developmental students, but make them feel they are learning in a college-level academic community. The exercises are designed to be challenging, yet engaging and accessible.

Paragraph Workbook

Table of Contents

Identifying Topic Sentence Errors

Identify each of the following as a title (T), an announcement (A), too broad (B), a supporting detail (SD) or a topic sentence (TS).

____ I want to discuss the perfume business.
____ Celebrities are finding the perfume industry to be a money-making venture.
____ A smelly business.
____ At $215,000 per bottle, Imperial Majesty is the world's most expensive perfume.
____ Perfume-making has undergone many changes since its beginnings in ancient Egypt.

____ A lack of Vitamin D can cause serious health problems.
____ Doctors estimate that up to 40% of the U.S. population is Vitamin D deficient.
____ This paragraph will explain how you can get enough Vitamin D through diet and exposure to sunlight.
____ Avoiding D deficiency.
____ Many vitamins are necessary for optimum health, and we can get these vitamins from a variety of sources.

____ A soccer player can take several precautions to reduce the risk of injury.
____ Pele, one of soccer's most famous players, retired more than 25 years ago.
____ I will explain how soccer has changed from a village free-for-all in medieval England to the game it is today.
____ Compared to other sports, soccer is much more exciting and interesting.
____ Soccer: an exciting alternative to baseball.

____ AKC dog events draw nearly two million entries annually.
____ Dog show judges look for specific "standards" in a particular breed.
____ The road to Best in Show.
____ This paragraph will describe how a dog can become a champion show dog.
____ Throughout history human beings and dogs have had many relationships.

____ Waking up to coffee
____ In this paragraph I will explain how a pope made coffee an acceptable drink for Europeans.
____ Seven million metric tons of coffee beans are harvested every year.
____ The growing, processing, shipping and marketing of coffee beans is an interesting process.
____ Pope Clement VIII was able to make coffee a respectable drink for Europeans.

____ President James Buchanan did little to prevent the Civil War.
____ James Buchanan the bachelor President
____ U.S. Presidents have dealt with many conflicts and handled them in different ways.
____ Buchanan was so disliked that his portrait was taken down from the Capitol rotunda to prevent it from being vandalized.
____ This paragraph tells about how little President Buchanan did to prevent the war between the states.

*For more practice with **topic sentences**, go to www.mywritinglab.com... MyWritingLab...**where better practice makes better writers!***

1

Composing Topic Sentences

For each of the following sets of details, write the topic sentence which they support. Remember that a topic sentence tells the limited subject and the controlling idea of a paragraph.

TS: _____
_____
_____

    a. Vitamin D deficiency can cause muscle weakness and pain often misdiagnosed as fibromyalgia.
    b. Without sufficient levels of vitamin D, the body cannot absorb calcium, which can lead to osteoporosis.
    c. A deficiency in Vitamin D can impair the body's ability to produce insulin.
    d. Rickets, a bone-wasting disease, is the result of severe vitamin D deficiency.

TS: _____
_____
_____

    a. Use art, font and layout to attract the eyes of newspaper browsers to your ad.
    b. Organize the ad clearly and logically, moving the reader from the headline to the description to the price to the seller contact information.
    c. Include specifics about your item such as the brand or model.
    d. Urge prospective buyers to act quickly, so they call you first.

TS: _____
_____
_____

    a. In the 1860s, actress Adah Isaacs Menken shocked theater critics by appearing on stage wearing a flesh-colored body stocking and riding a horse.
    b. Menken cut her hair short and smoked cigarettes in public during a time when respectable women did neither.
    c. Menken refused to perform on stage during Jewish holy days even at the height of her career.
    d. Menken married four men in seven years during a time when even one divorce could cause a scandal.

TS: _____
_____
_____

   a. Using tattooing equipment that has not been properly sterilized could lead to the transmission of Hepatitis B, syphilis, and even HIV.
   b. Tattoo ink is not regulated, and some people have experienced severe allergic reactions to it.
   c. The metallic pigment in some tattoos has caused people to experience pain and burning when they have MRIs.
   d. Infections can occur in new tattoos if appropriate aftercare is not followed.

TS: _____
_____
_____

   a. Named after the artist Salvador Dali, the Dali mustache is long and thin, curving upwards at the sides.
   b. With the Fu Manchu mustache, whiskers along the upper lip are grown very long and allowed to droop down each side of the mouth to the jaw.
   c. The Toothbrush mustache, thick and only about an inch wide, was made famous by Adolph Hitler and later Charlie Chaplin.
   d. The Handlebar mustache is bushy and grown long enough to curl the ends upwards with styling wax.

TS: _____
_____
_____

   a. Spuds Mackenzie, the white bull terrier mascot of Anheuser-Busch Beer, was so popular that an entire line of merchandise was designed around him.
   b. Nipper, the fox terrier, has been the longtime symbol of the RCA company.
   c. Taco Bell used a Spanish-speaking Chihuahua to sell tacos as well as millions of plush toy replicas of the popular dog.
   d. Even The National Crime Prevention Council chose a dog, McGruff, to promote its campaign of crime prevention.

*For more practice with **topic sentences**, go to www.mywritinglab.com... MyWritingLab...**where better practice makes better writers!***

Paragraph Unity

Circle the letters of the supporting details that do not support the following topic sentences.

1. TS: Abraham Lincoln's young son Tad could be a terror during the years he spent in the White House.

    a. Once when Lincoln was playing chess with a judge, Tad kicked the chess board, scattering pieces across the floor. Lincoln calmly took Tad's hand and went off to dinner with him.
    b. He broke a large mirror with his ball and ruined a marble table top by running his ink-covered fingers over the top of it.
    c. Tad begged his father to spare the life of their Thanksgiving turkey and turned it into a pet, leading it around the White House grounds on a string.
    d. Tad took tubes of paint from an artist who had come to paint Lincoln's portrait and smeared the paint all over the walls while his father looked on smiling.
    e. Tad once drove a team of goats through the East Room of the White House.
    f. Tad loved money, but he could not understand the difference between the size of a coin and its value. He preferred larger coins over small gold coins that were more valuable.

2. TS: Color can have an impact on both our mental and physical states.

    a. Perhaps because blue food is so rare, the color blue can cause people to lose their appetites.
    b. Red, however, is a popular food color, and restaurants often use a red color scheme because it stimulates people's appetites.
    c. In China, red symbolizes luck, so it is used in wedding ceremonies.
    d. Green is a calming color, which might be why many hospitals use green color schemes, and even surgeons wear green scrubs when operating.
    e. White is a popular color in fashion because it is neutral and can be worn with anything.
    f. Pink has a calming, almost tranquilizing effect, so some sports teams have painted the opposing team's locker room pink.

3. TS: Polar bears are particularly suited for life in the cold arctic regions.

    a. Because ice sheets are melting due to global warming, polar bears are not able to travel as far in their search for food.
    b. The polar bear's white coat makes it almost invisible as its stalks its prey.
    c. A single polar bear needs to eat between 50 and 75 seals per year to survive.
    d. Polar bears have black skin, which absorbs heat, and beneath their skin a layer of blubber keeps the bears well-insulated against the bitter cold.
    e. Soft bumps on the pads of their feet give polar bears the traction they need on slick ice.
    f. Polar bears have two layers of fur: an outer coat of long fur sticks together when wet to form a waterproof barrier, keeping the thick undercoat of fur dry.

4. TS: Wild animals can use tools in clever and innovative ways.

   a. Jane Goodall observed chimpanzees pick and trim long blades of grass, which they then poked into termite mounds to retrieve the tasty insects.
   b. Jane Goodall is considered the world's expert on chimpanzee behavior.
   c. Scientists have seen young animals learn to use tools by watching adults.
   d. Because the tasty ostrich egg has a shell too tough for them to peck open, Egyptian vultures have learned to throw rocks at the egg to crack it open.
   e. Green herons will drop a small object on the surface of water as "bait" and then snatch the fish that rises to the surface.
   f. Orangutans braid vines together to make a stronger rope.

5. TS: Wearing the number 13 has not been lucky for professional athletes.

   a. Pitcher Billy Wagner of the Houston Astros was hit on the side of the head by a line drive and later missed most of a season because of ligament surgery.
   b. Mats Sundin, captain of the Toronto Maple Leafs hockey team, was hit in the face by a puck, and needed fifteen stitches to close the gash between his eyes and forehead.
   c. Wilt Chamberlain is the only basketball player to have scored 100 points in a game and was named to 13 All-Star teams.
   d. Wearing the number 13 during the 1999 baseball season, pitcher Jeff Fassero compiled the worst single season ERA since 1937.
   e. Quarterback Dan Marino entered the Hall of Fame holding all-time records in passing touchdowns and passing yards.
   f. In addition to wearing the unlucky number, Brooklyn Dodger Pitcher Ralph Branca posed with a black cat before the 1951 play-offs where he would become famous for throwing the pitch that led to Bobby Thomson's famous home-run, "a shot heard around the world."

6. In 1905, Diamond Jim Brady, who had earned millions selling railroad equipment, gave an unforgettable party to honor his racehorse, Gold Heels.

   a. For seventeen hours, fifty guests consumed over $40,000 in food
   b. Another New York millionaire gave a dinner honoring his dog, which wore a $15,000 collar to the bash.
   c. Guests drank more than 500 bottles of champagne with their food.
   d. Although he was a voracious eater, Diamond Jim did not drink alcohol.
   e. For "party favors," ladies received diamond brooches, and men received diamond-studded watches.
   f. The entire affair, held at the Hoffman House in New York City, cost more than $100,000.

*For more practice with **paragraph unity**, go to www.mywritinglab.com... MyWritingLab...**where better practice makes better writers!***

Levels of Development

Part I. Rank the statements in the following sets according to their level of generalization with #1 being the most general and #3 being the least general.

____ a. Tony the Tiger has been roaring about the goodness of Kellogg's Sugar Frosted Flakes since 1952.

____ b. Advertisers often use animals to promote their products.

____ c. Cereal companies have had success using animated animals to promote breakfast cereals.

____ a. Caves provide three different types of habitats.

____ b. Bacteria and tiny multi-celled animals visible only through a microscope are all that can survive in the freezing ice caves of Greenland.

____ c. Glacial ice caves are perhaps the most challenging cave habitat.

____ a. When Arachne bragged that she was the greatest weaver, the goddess Athena turned her into a spider.

____ b. The Greek myths frequently warned people of the dangers of excessive pride.

____ c. Greek mythology explores a full range of interactions between gods and human beings.

____ a. Tidal energy can be used where there are large increases in tide.

____ b. A plant in France currently uses tidal energy to power more than 240,000 homes.

____ c. As the world looks for alternative sources of fuel, the ocean may be a boundless source of energy.

____ a. Wrestling can be more enjoyable and entertaining to watch if you understand how a match is scored.

____ b. If a wrestler cannot win his match by pinning his opponent, he must try to earn the most points in the match.

____ c. A wrestler can score five points by throwing his opponent in a high sweeping arc from a standing position to his back on the floor.

6

Part II. Each of the following sets should begin with the most general statement and end with the most specific statement. Add the missing level of development to each set.

1.   a. No matter what season of the year it is, the children in my neighborhood enjoy playing outside.

      b. _____
_____

      c. Despite the cold, they build snow forts and swoop down hills on their sleds.

2.   a. _____
_____

      b. Joe even puts caring for his car over his relationships.
      c. He broke up with one girlfriend because going to visit her was putting too many miles on his precious Mustang.

3.   a. College teachers hear a full range of excuses from students who miss class.
      b. Sometimes the weather provides the perfect excuse.
      c. _____
_____
_____

4.   a. Dieting can be especially difficult on special occasions.
      b. _____
_____

      c. Once the candles are blown out, I can't resist helping myself to a heaping plate of cake and ice cream.

5.   a. A date doesn't have to be an expensive night on the town.
      b. A local park can be the setting for an inexpensive but enjoyable date.
      c. _____
_____
_____

6.   a. Eric likes to use his appearance to shock people.
      b. Tattoos have become his latest means to draw attention to himself.
      c. _____
_____
_____

*For more practice with **paragraph development**, go to www.mywritinglab.com... MyWritingLab...**where better practice makes better writers!***

Developing a Paragraph with Reasons and Examples

Are you or is someone you know part of the Millennial Generation—those Americans born between 1980 and 2000? Complete the following outline to write a paragraph about the Millennials. First, determine which of the reasons listed below support the paragraph's main points and add them to the outline. Then use your personal knowledge of this generation to fill in specific supporting examples. Once the outline is complete, use it to write a paragraph about the Millennials, being sure to add transitions where they are appropriate.

.

TS: The Millennials—those Americans born between 1980 and 2000—have traits that make them a promising generation.

(First Main Idea) The Millennials are a confident generation.

(Reason)_____
_____

(Reason)_____
_____

(Example) _____
_____

(Second Main Idea) The Millennials are patriotic.

(Reason)_____
_____

(Reason)_____
_____

(Example) _____
_____

(Third Main Idea) Growing up in a multi-cultural world, the Millennials are inclusive.

(Reason)_____
_____

(Reason)_____
_____

(Example) _____
_____

Those growing up in the 90s and 00s have had more interaction with other ethnic groups and races than previous generations.

During the 1990s national attention to children was the highest it had been since the Baby Boomers were kids, and Millennials enjoyed the attention of involved, protective parents who sought to raise their children's self-esteem.

September 11, 2001 was a defining moment for the Millennials, and they were a part of the surge in nationalism and patriotism that followed.

In the workplace, Millennials tend to communicate more through technology than face-to-face.

Since they were toddlers, the Millennials have been told through their television shows that they are smart and special.

The Millennials are used to working in teams and have grown up with the notion that no one should be left behind.

A survey in 2001 showed that parents were most often named when Millennials were asked whom they most admired.

More Millennials are showing interest in politics and participation in political elections.

*For more practice with **paragraph development**, go to www.mywritinglab.com... MyWritingLab...**where better practice makes better writers!***

Analyzing Coherence in a Paragraph

Read the following paragraph carefully, noting the various ways the writer achieves coherence. Answer the questions that follow.

Space travel has evolved dramatically since the early '60s when John Glenn orbited the earth in a small Mercury capsule. In addition to improving the size, comfort and technological sophistication of the space vehicles, NASA has made eating in space a more enjoyable and tasty experience for astronauts. The first astronauts who tried to eat in the low gravity of a space vehicle squeezed their meals from tubes or sucked them up through straws. For chewing, there were cubes of dehydrated foods, moisturized and reconstituted by the astronaut's own saliva. Later, the Apollo astronauts, who journeyed to the moon, were the first to enjoy meals they could eat with a spoon. They injected water into a plastic container filled with their dehydrated meal and once wet, the food would stick to spoons. Apollo astronauts also ate food such as beef sandwiches and chocolate pudding kept moist in aluminum pouches called wetpacks. Beginning in the 1980s, astronauts aboard space shuttles could enjoy a wide variety of soups, casseroles, meats, fresh fruits and vegetables prepared in a galley equipped with a water dispenser for rehydrating foods and a convection oven for heating meals. In 2006, even this diverse menu was "kicked up a notch" by Chef Emeril Lagasse.   He designed a space menu for the Discovery astronauts that included jambalaya and bread pudding. NASA has plans for future space travelers to dine on fresh lettuce, spinach, rice and peanuts grown in special hydroponic systems aboard space vehicles bound for distant planets.

1. Coherence, the way a writer "connects" ideas in a paragraph, begins with a clear organizational strategy. Which of the following strategies does the writer of the space food paragraph use?
    __   chronological   ___ spatial   ___emphatic

2. What helps you determine that this is the organization strategy?

3. Give three examples of transitional words and phrases the writer uses.

    _____   _____   _____

4. A writer may also use pronouns to achieve coherence by having a pronoun refer back to an antecedent in a previous sentence. Find the two pronouns in this paragraph that refer to antecedents in the preceding sentence. Circle the pronoun and draw a line to the antecedent.

10

5. A writer also achieves coherence by repeating key words—nouns, adjectives and verbs. Give four examples of key words that are repeated in this paragraph.

   _____   _____   _____   _____

6. Sometimes, instead of repeating a word, a writer may use a synonym. What synonym for the key word *eat* does the writer use?

   _____

7. What synonym for *astronauts* does the writer use?

   _____

For more practice with **coherence**, *go to* www.mywritinglab.com... *MyWritingLab...***where better practice makes better writers!***

Paragraph Analysis

Read the following paragraph carefully and then match the instructor's comments to the sections of the paragraphs to which they refer.

The Most Famous Yell In The World

Perhaps the most famous yell in the world is the distinctive Tarzan yell used by Johnny Weissmuller in the Tarzan movies of the 1930s. Although there are stories about how the studio technicians created the yell by mixing a variety of sounds, Weissmuller claimed the yell was his own variation of the yodeling he had done as a young boy in Romania. Once he perfected the yell, technicians recorded it and for nearly fifty years used it in Tarzan movies. The yell was so famous and inspiring that during World War II it was broadcasted to the soldiers on the battlefront. Perhaps because he was so identified with his Tarzan yell, Weissmuller asked that a recording of the yell be played at his funeral. Weissmuller even said the yell once saved his life in 1959 when he was on his way to a golf tournament in Havana, Cuba. Castro's rebel forces had surrounded his car when Weissmuller cut loose with his famous yell. The soldiers immediately recognized the famous Tarzan, they escorted him safely to the tournament. In his later years, when Weissmuller attempted the yell, he would be hoarse for days. Long after Weissmuller's death, variations of the yell continue to show up. The comedian Carol Burnett, who had learned the yell as a child, frequently used it in her tv comedy show, which ran from 1967-'78. A variation of the yell was used in the movie *George of the Jungle.* The yell has also been heard in the James Bond film *Octopussy* and George Lucas's *Star Wars: Revenge of the Sith.*

1. Coherence—Are you using chronological order consistently?

2. This topic sentence shows a clear subject and controlling idea.

3. Sentence error—capitalization

4. Good transition

5. Good use of pronoun reference to achieve coherence

6. Unity—Does this support the idea that the yell is distinctive and well-known?

7. Nice repetition of key words

8. Ends a bit abruptly—conclusion?

9. Sentence error—comma splice

12

Analyzing a Description Paragraph

The following paragraph describes the ruins of Khara Khoto—or the Black City—which lies in the desolate Gobi desert of China. Read it carefully and answer the questions that follow.

In 1908, Colonel Pyotr Kuzmich Koslov, leader of a Russian Expedition to Mongolia, came upon the ruins of the lost city of Khara Khoto in the middle of the Gobi desert between China and Mongolia. The desolate, some say haunted, ruins of this desert city stand in silent testimony to the fragility of human settlement. Once a thriving Mongol city visited by Marco Polo, Khara Khoto had fertile fields where herds of cattle and camel grazed, and a life-giving river flowed right up to its massive walls. It was this river, according to local legends, that armies of the invading Ming Dynasty diverted away from the city in 1372. When the city's defenders grew weak by starvation and thirst under the relentless desert sun, the invaders breached the walls, sacked the city and massacred its inhabitants. Today, the Chinese say, the ghosts left by this merciless slaughter haunt the sand-filled streets and crumbling mud buildings. Tourists may come to gaze upon the twelve-foot thick outer city walls, the thirty-foot tall ramparts and the towers that still stand against the cloudless blue sky, but rarely does anyone venture into the dead city, even in the daylight. Even stories of a hoard of gold hidden by the doomed Mongol king do not entice adventure seekers. At night, only the wind stirs the sand that covers the shattered pottery, the bleached bones within the city walls.

> 1. Which adjectives best describe this desert city before the Ming invaders arrived?

> 2. Which words in this section of the paragraph work together to create a unified expression of the city as it is today?

3. This paragraph begins with the discovery of the city's ruins. Was this beginning an effective way to get the readers' attention? Why or why not?

4. The writer uses description to make a point about life, about the human condition. What is this point?

5. Explain how the writer incorporates the following rhetorical modes into this description paragraph: comparison/contrast and narration.

6. Some might argue that this paragraph ends abruptly. Write a sentence that clearly concludes the paragraph—perhaps by referring back to one of the opening sentences.

7. Circle the letter of the correct form for this paragraph's title.

    a. Ghosts in the Desert
    b. GHOSTS IN THE DESERT
    c. Ghosts In The Desert
    d. Ghosts in the desert

Building a Description Paragraph

Write a paragraph that describes a place you know well. In addition to using descriptive sensory details to create a vivid impression of this place for your reader, use the description of this place to make a point about people—i.e. the human condition. The description of Kara Khoto, for example, made the point that our place on earth can be very fragile, very temporary. Write this paragraph for your peers whom you want to engage and interest with your descriptive details while giving them a new insight into the meaning of a place.

Step #1—Brainstorming
First, brainstorm as many sensory details about this place as you can. Use the five senses as a way to think of descriptive details. While you may not have details for every sense, try to think of as many as you can.

Place: _____

sight	sound	taste	touch	smell

After looking at the sensory details you've brainstormed, now try to brainstorm some insights this place might give about people, their behaviors, their hopes or dreams, their strengths, their weaknesses.

_____

_____

_____

_____

_____

14

Step #2—Organizing Compose a topic sentence and a scratch outline to help organize the details you will use in this paragraph.

Topic Sentence:_____
_____

Consider using a spatial organization—present the details as a person moving through physical space would encounter them.

_____
_____
_____
_____

Step #3—Drafting Write a first draft of this paragraph.

Step #4—Analyze the Draft for Revision and Revise

1. According to your topic sentence, this paragraph will describe
_____ to make the following point about people:_____
_____.

2. Do all of your sentences stay focused on this subject and support its point? Place a check by any sentences that seem to stray off track.

3. Give two examples of key words you repeat in this paragraph.

_____   _____

4. Give three examples of transitions you use in this paragraph.
_____   _____   _____

5. What descriptive details have you chosen to make your points more striking and memorable for the reader?

_____
_____
_____

6. What have you done to give the reader a new way of looking at or thinking about this place?

7. Have you used other rhetorical strategies—comparison/contrast, narration, definition—in this description? What are they and how are they used in the description?

8. How does the last sentence in your paragraph indicate a clear ending?

9. Based on your responses to these questions, what are the main revisions you plan to make to your draft?

Step #5—Edit Revised Draft

For more practice with **description**, *go to* www.mywritinglab.com... *MyWritingLab...* **where better practice makes better writers!**

Analyzing a Narrative Paragraph

A narrative tells a story that often offers some insights into people we will never meet and experiences we will never have ourselves. Such narratives may satisfy our curiosity or help us better understand why people behave the way they do.

The following narrative is about Robert Pershing Wadlow, better known as the Alton Giant. At the time of his death in 1940, Wadlow was 8'11.1" tall, making him the tallest person in history according to the Guinness Book of World Records. A quiet, somewhat shy man, Wadlow spent his short life in Alton, Illinois, when he wasn't traveling with his father promoting a shoe company that provided him with his own size 37 AAA shoes. Read the paragraph carefully and answer the questions that follow.

When Robert Wadlow was twenty-years-old, he and his father set out on a countrywide promotional tour for a shoe company. After his father removed the front passenger seat of the family car, Robert climbed in the back seat, stretching out his long legs, and the two of them set off on a 300,000 mile tour to over 800 towns in 41 states. During one stop in Hot Springs, Arkansas, Robert and Mr. Wadlow decided to go with some friends to see a night club show. A friend called ahead for reservations and was told that men attending the show were required to wear a coat or jacket. Knowing that Robert had not packed a coat or jacket for a trip to Arkansas in sweltering summer heat, the friend said that the group had a young man who did not have proper attire. He was reassured that the club provided "loaners" for such patrons. "But this is a 'big' boy," the friend tried to explain. Again he was reassured that the club had big coats and jackets to loan to patrons. When Robert arrived at the club with his father and friends, the host could only stare at the 8'11" gentle giant who weighed over four hundred pounds and stammer, "He *is* a big boy, isn't he." Robert was able to see the show without a coat or jacket.

1. This paragraph does not have an explicit topic sentence. How does the writer still keep the paragraph unified? What point does the paragraph make about rules?

2. What does this incident help you understand about Robert Wadlow? What do you learn about the people who met Robert?

3. Why doesn't this paragraph go on to discuss more of the experiences Robert and his father had on the tour?

17

4. A narrative follows a chronological order. Underline the transitional words and phrases the writer uses to connect the parts of the story.

5. What details make the experience described here more vivid for the readers?

6. What would be a good title for this paragraph? Be sure to capitalize the title properly.

Building a Narrative Paragraph

The story about Robert Wadlow described how an exception to a rule was made because of special circumstances. Situations like this occur often in life. Parents may allow their teenager to stay out past curfew because of a special event. A teacher may extend the deadline for an assignment for a particular student. Perhaps a boss bends company policy to help out an employee. Write a paragraph that tells of a time you made an exception to a rule or an exception was made for you. Your audience for this paragraph is your peers who are interested in knowing what kinds of circumstances allow for "bending the rules."

Step #1—Freewriting and Asking the Journalist's Questions You might begin by freewriting about several times you were involved in this kind of situation. Once you can focus on one memorable incident —one that can be adequately covered in a single paragraph—do a bit of more focused freewriting on some of the questions journalists use to be sure to cover all the important elements of a good story. The following prompts will help you.

When? Where?	What? How?	Who?	Why?
Setting—When and where does this incident take place? What details are most important to establish this setting?	**Plot**—What is the conflict that needs to be resolved in this story? What is the rule and why does an exception need to be made? How will I create a sense of curiosity or anticipation in my readers?	**Characters**—Who are the principal characters involved in this incident? What traits do these characters have that I want the narrative to reveal? Can I use short dialogue to reveal character and move the story along?	**Theme or Point of the narrative**—Why is this story important? What do I want my readers to better understand about "bending rules"? Should we always be willing to make exceptions? Are the consequences always good? Will I state this point in an explicit thesis, or will I let the story convey the point implicitly?

19

Step #2—Organizing   State the point you want your story to make even if you chose not to state it explicitly in your paragraph. Then use a chronological order to sketch out the main parts of the story.

Point: _____

_____

_____

_____

_____

_____

Step #3—Drafting   Write a first draft of this paragraph.

Step #4—Analyze the Draft for Revision and Revise

1. Did you decide to state the point of your story explicitly? If so, which sentence makes that point? If you have decided to imply the point of the story, what have you done to make sure the reader will understand your point?

2. A narrative paragraph cannot try to do too much, or the story can get lost in too many details. Are there any details in your narrative that detract from the main point of your story?

3. Give two examples of key words you repeat in this paragraph.

    _____   _____

4. Give two examples of transitions you use in this paragraph to help the reader follow the chronological order.

    _____   _____

20

5. Give two examples of specific details you include to make the story more vivid for the readers.

6. Did you use dialogue? If so, does the statement help move the plot along or does it reveal something important about the character making the statement? How?

7. Does the story come to a clear end? Are there any loose ends that might leave your readers wondering about something that was not included?

8. Based on your responses to these questions, what are the main revisions you plan to make to your draft?

Step #5—Edit Revised Draft

*For more practice with **narration**, go to www.mywritinglab.com... MyWritingLab...**where better practice makes better writers!***

Analyzing an Illustration Paragraph

An illustration paragraph uses examples to "show" the writer's point about the subject. The following paragraph shows what a compulsive gambler John Warne Gates, a turn-of-the-century millionaire businessman, was. Read it carefully and answer the questions that follow.

<table>
<tr>
<td>

1. What does the writer do to generate the readers' interest in the subject?

</td>
<td>

John Warne Gates was an astute businessman, a speculator who competed with financial giants like J.P. Morgan and Andrew Carnegie. However, Gates is best remembered for his compulsive, no-holds-barred gambling that earned him the nickname "Bet-A-Million." Gates's obsession with gambling began when he was a schoolboy in Turner's Junction, where he played poker with railroad workers.

</td>
</tr>
</table>

John Warne Gates was an astute businessman, a speculator who competed with financial giants like J.P. Morgan and Andrew Carnegie. However, Gates is best remembered for his compulsive, no-holds-barred gambling that earned him the nickname "Bet-A-Million." Gates's obsession with gambling began when he was a schoolboy in Turner's Junction, where he played poker with railroad workers. As an adult, Gates might lose a million dollars in poker marathons that lasted several days, but he always won more than he lost. And he was a fearless gambler, earning his nickname by trying to place a million dollar bet on a horse at the Saratoga race track. If horses, cards, dice and roulette were not around, Gates would bet on anything available. Once a Kansas City sports writer, representing a syndicate, placed a $40,000 wager on any game Gates chose. Gates flipped a gold piece and asked the writer to call "Heads or tails." The writer then became known as the man who lost $40,000 in ten seconds to Bet-A-Million Gates. Wealthy playboy John Drake also lost a small fortune to Gates in an impulsive wager. Each man dunked a piece of bread in his coffee and then set the bread on the table to attract flies. The one whose bread attracted the most flies would win $1,000 per fly. Gates won a small fortune probably because he had sweetened his coffee with six cubes of sugar before dunking his bread. It was the same shrewd gambling spirit that later led Gates to make millions in Texas oil speculations before his death in 1911.

1. What does the writer do to generate the readers' interest in the subject?

2. What two coherence devices are combined here?

3. What are some of the specific details the writer includes here to make the examples more vivid and interesting?

4. How does this key word connect the conclusion to the introduction and bring the paragraph full circle?

5. The author uses examples to show that Gates was a gambler. How do these examples also show that Gates was "fearless" and "compulsive"?

6. What would be a good title for this paragraph? Be sure to capitalize the title properly.

Building an Illustration Paragraph

The examples of John Warne Gates's gambling exploits makes his character vivid for readers who will never know him personally. Choose a person you know who has a striking behavior and write a paragraph that uses examples to vividly *show* that behavior. Your readers are peers who do not know this person but who would enjoy reading about an interesting character.

Step #1—Freewriting and Mapping First, freewrite about a person you know who has a distinctive behavior. Try to generate as many examples of that behavior as you can. Then use the following map to flesh out the examples with same specific details.

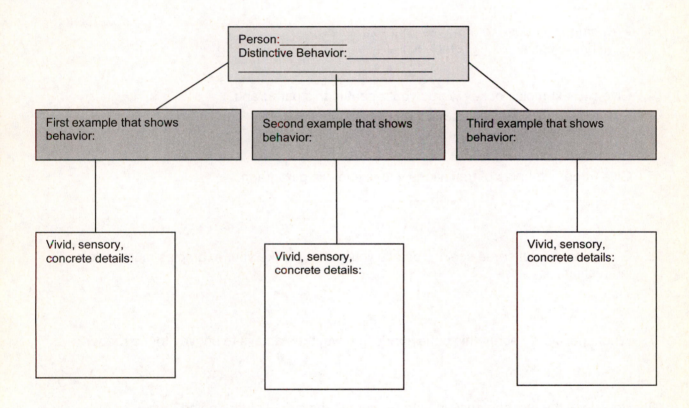

Step #2—Organizing Compose a topic sentence and use the following scratch outline to help organize the examples you will use in this paragraph.

Topic Sentence: _____

_____

Example 1_____

Example 2_____

Example 3_____

23

Step #3—Drafting   Write a first draft of this paragraph.

Step #4—Analyze the Draft for Revision and Revise

1. According to your topic sentence, the subject of this paragraph is
   _____ and the behavior you want to illustrate is
   _____.

2. Do all of your sentences stay focused on this subject and illustrate this behavior? Place a check by any sentences that seem to stray off track.

3. How did you choose to organize your examples?
   ___ chronological   ___ emphatic

4. Give two examples of key words you repeat in this paragraph.
   _____   _____

5. Give three examples of transitions you use in this paragraph.
   _____   _____   _____

6. Give examples of some specific details you used to make your examples more vivid and interesting.

7. What specifically about this behavior do you want the details to convey to the reader?

8. How does the last sentence in your paragraph indicate a clear ending?

9. Based on your responses to these questions, what are the main revisions you plan to make to your draft?

Step #5—Edit Revised Draft

*For more practice with **illustration**, go to www.mywritinglab.com... MyWritingLab...**where better practice makes better writers!***

24

Analyzing a Process Paragraph

The following paragraph describes foot binding, a custom that began in China nearly a thousand years ago and continued up until the early 1900s. Read it carefully and answer the questions that follow.

For several centuries, women in China had their feet bound in order to achieve their culture's ideal of beauty. This process of binding the feet to stunt their growth was both painful and dangerous. When a Chinese girl was four to six years old, her mother would begin the foot binding process during the winter months when the cold could help numb the pain. After having her feet soaked in warm water or animal blood, the young girl would have her toe nails cut very short to prevent them from growing into the flesh of her foot. Then the mother would massage her daughter's feet before breaking the four smallest toes on each foot. Even greater pain followed when the mother would wrap about ten feet of silk or cotton bandages around the girl's toes and pull them tightly, bending the ball of the foot to the heel. Every two days the bandages would be removed, rebound and pulled even tighter. Following two years of this process, a girl's feet were only three to four inches long. During this time, pain was constant, serious infection was common and even death from infection was a possibility.

1. Underline the topic sentence of this paragraph. According to this topic sentence, the subject or topic of the paragraph is _____, and the point the writer wants to make is _____ .

2. Which organizational pattern does this paragraph follow?

    ___ chronological ___ spatial ___ emphatic

3. Give two examples of key words that are repeated in this paragraph.

    _____   _____

4. Give three examples of transitional words or phrases used in this paragraph.

   _____   _____   _____

5. Give two examples of specific details the writer uses in this paragraph.

   _____   _____

6. Which of the following would be the best title for this paragraph?

   a. A Process Paragraph
   b. Foot Binding in China
   c. A Painful Practice
   d. The Painful Price for Beauty

Building a Process Paragraph

Being good listeners is especially important for college students who are often tested over information presented in lectures. Using your own experiences and some of the following ideas already brainstormed, write a process paragraph entitled "How to Get the Most out of a College Lecture." Imagine your audience for this paragraph will be first semester college freshmen who have not yet attended their first lecture.

Step #1--Brainstorming   Add your own ideas and examples* to this list.

> *Personal examples can add interest and clarity to writing. Try to include examples of your own listening and note-taking strategies in specific classes.

sit close enough to see and hear the instructor
make a commitment to be a better listener
don't try to write down everything
come prepared to the lecture
keep an open mind
try to identify the key ideas
review notes
resist distractions
read assignments before class
listen for signal words like "It is important to remember..." "There are three reasons..."
have a couple pens and paper for notes
use the reading assignment to set up questions for the lecture to answer
resist daydreaming—summarize and anticipate
respond to the instructor—ask questions, laugh when appropriate, eye contact

_____

_____

_____

_____

_____

_____

Step #2—Organizing   Compose a topic sentence and use the following scratch outline to help organize the points you will use in this paragraph.

Topic Sentence: _____

_____

Before the lecture

During the lecture

Following the lecture

Step #3—Drafting Write a first draft of this paragraph.

Step #4—Analyze the Draft for Revision and Revise

1. According to your topic sentence, the subject of this paragraph is
   _____ and the point you want to make about this subject is
   _____.

2. Do all of your sentences stay focused on this subject and support its point? Place a check by any sentences that seem to stray off track.

3. What organizational strategy does this paragraph follow?
   ___ chronological   ___spatial   ___emphatic

4. Give two examples of key words you repeat in this paragraph.
   _____   _____

5. Give three examples of transitions you use in this paragraph.
   _____   _____   _____

6. Give an example of a specific detail you use that will be particularly helpful for someone following this process.

7. Give an example of a personal example you use in this paragraph that adds interest and clarity.

8. What in your paragraph might be confusing to someone who has never attended a college-level lecture?

9. How does the last sentence in your paragraph indicate a clear ending to the process you've described?

10. Based on your responses to these questions, what are the main revisions you plan to make to your draft?

Step #5—Edit Revised Draft

*For more practice with **process**, go to www.mywritinglab.com... MyWritingLab...**where better practice makes better writers!***

Analyzing a Comparison/Contrast Paragraph

The following paragraph compares the historical Jesse James to the Jesse James often depicted in movies and books. Read the paragraph carefully and then label the parts as indicated.

Despite the romanticized story of his life in movies and books, the outlaw Jesse James was not a heroic, western Robin Hood. One myth about Jesse James is that he and his brother, Frank, robbed the railroads because the railroad companies forced the brothers off their land. In reality, the railroads were already established in the area when the James brothers began holding up and robbing trains. It's more likely the James brothers began robbing trains because banks had increased security and began using time lock vaults. Nor was Jesse James forced into crime because as a Southern sympathizer, he could not find work after the Civil War. Although times were hard following the war, James had uncles in Kansas City who were successful businessmen willing to help out family members by giving them jobs. Jesse James chose robbery as a way of life; he was not forced into it. An even bigger myth is that James robbed from the rich and gave to the poor. The local banks James robbed were not federally insured, so the townspeople and farmers lost money. And when the James gang robbed a train or stage coach, they took money from anyone who happened to be aboard. In the course of fifteen years, the James gang committed at least twenty-six hold-ups, made off with more than $200,000 and killed at least seventeen men, some unarmed and some innocent by-standers. The only ones who benefited financially from these crimes were the robbers' families. Far from being a Robin Hood, Jesse James stole from anyone and kept the money for himself.

1. Identify the following: the topic sentence
   four transitions
   a repeated key word
   specific details
   a synonym for *robberies*

2. Besides showing that the real Jesse James is not the same man depicted in movies and books, what larger point or lesson might be seen in this paragraph?

3. This comparison/contrast paragraph follows a point-by-point pattern. Rewrite it using a block pattern of organization.

4. Which title best fits this paragraph?

   a. Looking at Truth and Legend
   b. A Famous Robber
   c. Jesse James: Hero or Criminal?
   d. Jesse James

Building a Comparison/Contrast Paragraph

Step #1—Brainstorming   Choose <u>one</u> of the following lists of customs and brainstorm a corresponding list of the customs in your culture.   Your goal is to write a paragraph that shows similarities and/or differences between cultures. Imagine that you reader knows your culture but knows nothing about the other culture. You do not need to include every detail or example given in the lists. Choose what you think are the most interesting and informative.

Dining in Hong Kong

Arrive on time for dinner
Often a seating plan
Host will announce when to begin eating
Food often served on revolving tray
Try everything
Never eat last piece from serving tray
Place chopsticks on rest after every few
      bites and when speaking
Do not appear gluttonous:
      refuse second serving at least once
      always leave some food in your bowl
Place chopsticks on rest or on table, never
      across bowl
Burping is considered a compliment
Typical meal:
      drink—Sake
      rice
      smoked duck, kung pao chicken,
      twice-cooked pork, or *mapo dofu,*
      which is tofu and minced meat

Business Meeting in Saudi Arabia

Always make appointments a few weeks to a
    month in advance
Meetings usually in morning
Important to arrive on time but it's customary to
      keep foreigners waiting
Prefer to deal with known and trusted people—
      take time to build relationship
Begin with small talk about health and families,
      but never inquire about a Saudi's wife
Meetings often interrupted when others come
      into room and start new conversations
Decisions made slowly, requiring several layers
      of approval and several visits
Final decisions made by highest-ranking person
Repeating main points is seen as being truthful
Dislike high pressure tactics
Compromise necessary if someone's dignity is
      an issue
Saudis avoid giving bad news and saying "yes"
      may mean only "maybe"

Greetings in Kenya

Common greeting –handshake
Wait for woman to extend hand first
Handshake longer for friends than others
Show respect to elders and those of higher
      status by grasping the right wrist with
      the left hand while shaking hands
Lower eyes when greeting an elder or one of
      higher status
Ask questions about health, family, business
      Bad manners to skip this or rush it
Titles important—use academic, professional or
      honorific title followed by surname
Women over 21 addressed as "Mama"
Men over 35 addressed as "Mzee"
Children refer to all adults as Aunt or Uncle

Your List (Compare your culture to one of the three listed scenarios such as "Greetings in the United States.")

_____ in _____

Step #2—Organizing Compose a topic sentence that includes what is being compared and/or contrasted and the significance of knowing these similarities and/or differences. Decide whether to use a block or a point-by-point pattern of organization.

TS _____

1st Culture
    a. _____
    b. _____
    c. _____
    d. _____
2nd Culture
    a. _____
    b. _____
    c. _____
    d. _____

TS _____

I _____
    Culture 1
    Culture 2

II _____
    Culture 1
    Culture 2

III _____
    Culture 1
    Culture 2

IV _____
    Culture 1
    Culture 2

Step #3—Drafting Write a first draft of this paragraph.

Step #4—Analyze the Draft for Revision and Revise

1. According to your topic sentence, You are comparing _____ and _____ with an emphasis on (similarities/differences/both) to show that _____ .

2. Do all of your sentences stay focused on this subject and support its point? Place a check by any sentences that seem to stray off track.

3. What organizational strategy does this paragraph follow?

    __block   __point-by-point

4. Give two examples of key words you repeat in this paragraph.
    _____   _____

5. Give three examples of transitions you use in this paragraph.
    _____ _____ _____

32

6. Which difference between the two cultures do you think the reader will find most interesting or informative? How have you emphasized or highlighted this difference?

7. How does the last sentence in your paragraph indicate a clear ending?

8. Based on your responses to these questions, what are the main revisions you plan to make to your draft?

Step #5—Edit Revised Draft

*For more practice with **comparison and contrast**, go to www.mywritinglab.com... MyWritingLab...**where better practice makes better writers!***

Analyzing a Cause and Effect Paragraph

The following paragraph tells some of the reasons (causes) people are fired from their jobs. Read the paragraph carefully and answer the questions that follow.

Getting fired often involves ignoring some basic expectations. Employers expect their employees to know how to do the work they were hired to do. Those employees who overstated their experience or qualifications during a job interview may find themselves fired if they cannot quickly learn their jobs. Similarly, frustrated employers will fire those who work too slowly and make frequent errors. Employers also expect employees to get along with their colleagues. While some people have more social skills than others, all employees can show respect towards their co-workers. Most employers will not tolerate employees who spread malicious gossip, blame colleagues for problems, and behave rudely toward others. Perhaps the most important expectation employers have is honesty. Employees who falsify time sheets, expense reports and project reports nearly always face termination when they are caught. Stealing company materials and equipment is grounds for dismissal as well as using company resources and time for non-company business. Employers expect employees to be qualified, personable and honest. Someone not meeting these expectations will soon hear the dreaded words, "You're fired!"

1. Underline the topic sentence. According to this topic sentence, the effect is
   _____ , which is caused by _____ .

2. Which organizational pattern does this paragraph follow?
   __ chronological   __ spatial   __ emphatic

3. Give three examples of key words that are repeated.
   _____   _____   _____

4. What word is a synonym for *colleagues*?
   _____

5. Give three examples of transitional words or phrases.
   _____   _____   _____

6. Circle the letter that shows the correct form of the title of this paragraph.
   a. HOW TO GET FIRED
   b. How To Get Fired
   c. How to Get Fired
   d. How to get Fired

Building a Cause and Effect Paragraph

While young people find many positive benefits from participating in sports, some negative consequences can also result, especially when a young person pushes too hard to be successful in a single sport. Add your own ideas and examples to the following map to generate enough prewriting for a paragraph entitled "Falling Stars: The Downside of Youth Athletics." Imagine that your audience for this paragraph will be parents of student athletes.

Step #1--Mapping

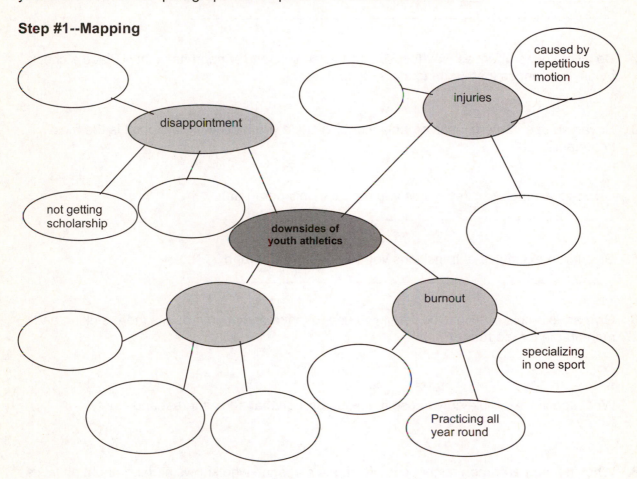

Step #2—Organizing Compose a topic sentence and a scratch outline to help organize the points you will use in this paragraph. Consider using emphatic order, moving from the least to the most harmful consequence.

Topic Sentence: _____

_____

least harmful effect: _____

effect: _____

effect: _____

most harmful effect: _____

35

Step #3—Drafting   Write a first draft of this paragraph.

Step #4—Analyze the Draft for Revision and Revise

1. According to your topic sentence, the subject of this paragraph is
   _____ and the point you want to make about this subject is
   _____.

2. Do all of your sentences stay focused on this subject and support its point? Place a check by any sentences that seem to stray off track.

3. Have you used an emphatic organization? Why do you think your last point is the most important?

4. Give two examples of key words you repeat in this paragraph.
   _____   _____

5. Give three examples of transitions you use in this paragraph.
   _____   _____   _____

6. Give an example of a specific detail you use to make one of your points more striking and memorable for the reader.

7. What specific example do you use in this paragraph that adds interest and clarity?

8. What in your paragraph might be confusing to someone who knows nothing about athletics for young people?

9. How does the last sentence in your paragraph indicate a clear ending?

10. Based on your responses to these questions, what are the main revisions you plan to make to your draft?

Step #5—Edit Revised Draft

*For more practice with **cause and effect**, go to www.mywritinglab.com... MyWritingLab...**where better practice makes better writers!***

Analyzing a Classification Paragraph

Dog shows have grown increasingly popular, and the most recent Best in Show winner of the prestigious Westminster Kennel Club dog show, a beagle named Uno, has become a celebrity, even appearing on talk shows. Before Uno could compete for Best in Show, he had to win Best in Breed by competing against other beagles. He then had to win the Group competition. The following paragraph discusses the various groups of dogs designated by the American Kennel Club (AKC). Read it carefully and answer the questions that follow.

The American Kennel Club (AKC) recognizes over 150 breeds of dogs, and has classified these dogs into seven groups for competing in dog shows. The first group, called the Sporting Group, consists of dogs bred specifically to help hunters flush and retrieve game. These energetic, even-tempered dogs include such breeds as Labrador retrievers and Irish setters. Also known to be excellent hunting dogs, hounds were given their own group, the Hound Group, in 1930. The breeds in this group range in size from the Irish wolfhound to the beagle and dachshund. Most hounds are known for their superior sense of smell and habit of baying loudly when on the trail of game. Some of the strongest and most intelligent dogs fall into the Working Group. Dogs such as the St. Bernard, the mastiff, the great dane and the Siberian husky were bred to guard property, to pull carts and sleds and to engage in rescue work. Feisty, strong-willed terriers make up the fourth group. Breeds in the Terrier Group were originally bred to hunt and kill vermin, though today few owners of Airedales, schnauzers and Scottish terriers send their dogs after rats. Dogs bred to be small, loving companions make up the Toy Group. Understandably, some of the most popular breeds of pets—toy poodles, Chihuahuas, Yorkshire terriers and Pomeranians—make up this group. The sixth group, the Non-Sporting Group, is a mixed bag of breeds, diverse in size, temperament and function. Bulldogs, Dalmatians, standard poodles and Lhasa apsos are among the dogs in this group. The last group consists of dogs bred for their ability to herd other animals. The collie, German shepherd, Welsh corgi and Australian cattle dogs are all members of the Herding Group. In the world of competitive all-breed dog shows, only those dogs that have won in their group can go on to compete to be Best in Show.

1.   Most things can be classified, or put into groups, on the basis of different criteria or ruling principles. Upon what does the American Kennel Club base its classification of dogs?

2. When using classification, writers can sometimes fall into the trap of using redundant sentence structures and predictable transitions: "The first category of dogs is the Sporting Group. . . . The second category of dogs is the Hound Group. . . . The third category of dogs is the Working Group. . . . and so on." What does this writer do to keep the sentences varied and the paragraph coherent?

3. Give three examples of key words that the writer repeats.

   _____   _____   _____

4. Give examples of three transitional words or phrases the writer uses.

   _____   _____   _____

5. Besides examples of the breeds in each group, what other examples does the writer use to clarify the distinctions among the various groups of dogs?

6. How does the concluding sentence relate back to the first sentence in the paragraph?

7. What would be a good title for this paragraph?

38

Building a Classification Paragraph

The pet industry is a multi-million dollar one here in the United States, and there are many ways one could look at our nation's obsession with pets. For this paragraph, classify pet owners according to the pets they have. After reading about the AKC's grouping of dogs for show purposes, you may already have noticed some reasons for having pets. Use the following map, which has been started for you, to come up with more reasons for having pets.

Make the paragraph informative and interesting by adding examples from your own experiences. For example, if you know someone who raises parakeets and sells some of the young birds for extra household income, you could include that example to illustrate how some people keep pets as a way to earn money. Do, however, keep in mind that we are talking about animals kept primarily as pets. You would not include farm animals, nor would you consider minks raised on a farm to supply the fur industry as "pets." Your audience for this paragraph is peers who may not have thought about the many roles pets play in people's lives.

Step #1—Mapping

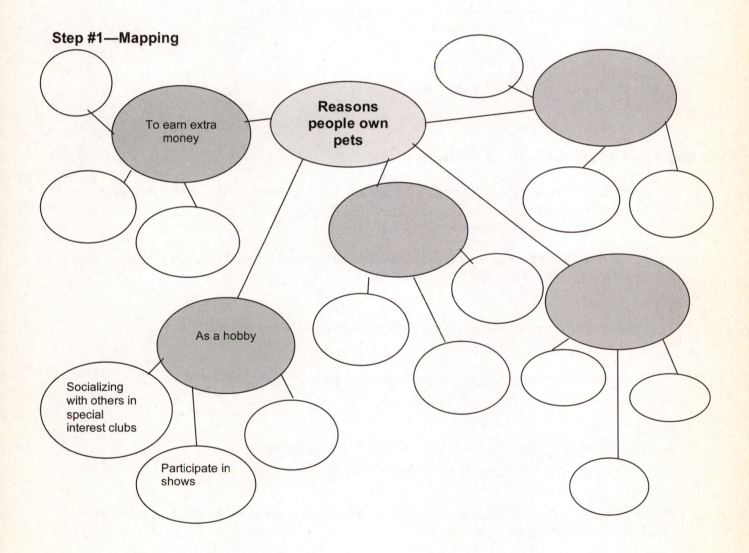

Step #2—Organizing Compose a topic sentence that indicates what you have classified (pet owners), the basis or ruling principle of your classification (reasons people own them) and the point you want this classification to make. (What can we learn or better understand by looking closely at all the reasons people own pets?) Avoid a topic sentence that simply states "People own pets for many reasons."

Once you have a topic sentence, organize your categories in the order the paragraph will discuss them. You may have more or less than five categories.

Topic Sentence:_____

_____

Category #1_____

Category #2_____

Category #3_____

Category #4_____

Category #5_____

Step #3—Drafting   Write a first draft of this paragraph.

Step #4—Analyze the Draft for Revision and Revise

1. According to your topic sentence, the point you want to make about this classification of pet owners is _____.

2. Do all of your sentences stay focused on this subject and support its point? Place a check by any sentences that seem to stray off track.

3. Why did you choose to present the categories in this particular order?

4. Give two examples of key words you repeat in this paragraph.
_____   _____

5. Give three examples of transitions you use in this paragraph.
_____   _____   _____

6. What did you do to keep your transitions from being a monotonous "The first category. . . The second category. . . and so on?

7. Give two examples of specific details you use to make your categories more striking and memorable for the reader.

8. What specific example do you use in this paragraph that adds interest and clarity?

9. Look at the details and examples you have presented for each category. How have you kept the presentation of the material from sounding repetitious and monotonous?

10. How does the last sentence in your paragraph indicate a clear ending?

11. Based on your responses to these questions, what are the main revisions you plan to make to your draft?

Step #5—Edit Revised Draft

For more practice with **classification**, *go to* www.mywritinglab.com... *MyWritingLab...**where better practice makes better writers!***

Analyzing a Definition Paragraph

The following paragraph defines celiac disease, a disorder affecting over two million Americans. Read it carefully and answer the questions that follow.

You may have noticed a section in your grocery store that carries products labeled "gluten-free." While anyone may eat and enjoy gluten-free foods, for people with celiac disease, these foods offer healthy alternatives to many foods most of us take for granted. Can you imagine never being able to eat anything with wheat, barley or rye ingredients? Along with cakes, cookies and other bakery items, you couldn't eat a wide variety of processed food ranging from pasta and potato chips to cold cuts because they contain wheat and wheat by-products. For people with celiac disease, such a restrictive diet is a life-long necessity for good health because their bodies cannot tolerate the protein gluten, which is found in wheat, barley and rye. When people with celiac disease eat gluten, they seriously damage their small intestines, and food cannot be absorbed into the bloodstream, resulting in malnutrition no matter how much food is eaten. In addition to malnutrition, people with untreated celiac disease are at risk for anemia, osteoporosis, seizures and cancer. Even the early symptoms of celiac disease can be painful or unpleasant, including stomach bloating, gas, chronic diarrhea or constipation, joint pain, irritability and fatigue. For the estimated 1 in 133 Americans with celiac disease, only a lifelong gluten-free diet offers the chance for a healthy life.

1. This paragraph defines celiac disease. What else does it define?

2. What does the writer do to generate interest in readers who do not have this disease or who may know nothing about it?

3. What specific examples in this paragraph help to clarify the terms being defined or explained?

4. Underline the words and phrases that help the organization or flow of ideas in this paragraph.

5. What other information about celiac disease might have been included in this paragraph to help the readers' understanding of this disease?

6. Which of the following titles is properly capitalized?

    a. Eating For Life With Celiac Disease
    b. EATING FOR LIFE WITH CELIAC DISEASE
    c. Eating for Life With Celiac Disease
    d. Eating for Life with Celiac Disease

Building a Definition Paragraph

Many people are fascinated by stories of Big Foot or the Loch Ness monster. Those who try to verify the existence of such creatures by gathering evidence are called *cryptozoologists*. Use the following information and your own ideas to write an organized paragraph that defines *cryptozoology* for someone who has never heard of the term before. Remember, you may not need to use all the information generated in prewriting. Choose the points and examples you think are best.

Step #1—Mapping and Brainstorming

Criptids = animals that might exist not accepted by modern science
Zoologist = one who studies animals
Cryptozoology—study of animals not formally recognized by science

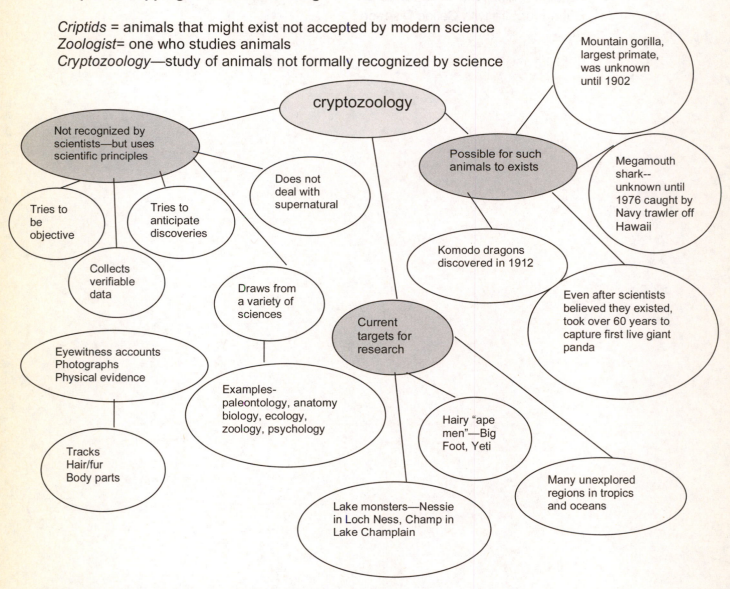

No degree programs, few college-level courses
No "real" jobs for scientists with cryptozoological interests
Why study it?—fascination with unknown
　　　　　　love of mystery, thrill of discovery

44

Step #2—Organizing Compose a topic sentence and a scratch outline to help organize the points you will use in this paragraph.

What questions should a definition paragraph about cryptozoology answer?

_____ ?
_____ ?
_____ ?
_____ ?
_____ ?

What would be a logical way to organize responses to these questions? Chronological? Spatial? Emphatic?

TS _____
_____

I. _____
II. _____
III. _____
IV. _____
V. _____

Step #3—Drafting   Write a first draft of this paragraph.

Step #4—Analyze the Draft for Revision and Revise

1. According to your topic sentence, the subject of this paragraph is
_____ and the point you want to make about this subject is
_____.

2. Do all of your sentences stay focused on this subject and support its point? Place a check by any sentences that seem to stray off track.

3. Give two examples of key words you repeat in this paragraph.

_____   _____

4. Have you clearly connected the "parts" of this definition so the paragraph flows easily for the reader to follow? How have you done this?

45

5. Give three examples of transitions you use in this paragraph.
   _____   _____   _____

6. What examples have you chosen to make your points more striking and memorable for the reader?
   _____
   _____
   _____

7. What in your paragraph might still be confusing to someone who knows nothing about cryptozoology? Where could you go to find more information on this subject?

8. What part of this paragraph do you think the reader will find the most interesting or informative?

9. How does the last sentence in your paragraph indicate a clear ending?

10. Based on your responses to these questions, what are the main revisions you plan to make to your draft?

Step #5—Edit Revised Draft

For more practice with **definition**, *go to* www.mywritinglab.com... *MyWritingLab...**where better practice makes better writers!***

46

Analyzing a Persuasion Paragraph

A persuasion paragraph offers convincing evidence in order to take a stand on a controversial subject. In this paragraph, the writer looks at what many consumers do not consider: how food is processed before being brought to the grocery store and labeled. Read the following paragraph carefully and answer the questions that follow.

We often hear groceries and restaurants tout their beef products as coming from "corn-fed" cattle. The implication is that this meat is more wholesome and good. However, being corn-fed is not healthy for the cattle, and eating corn-fed cattle may not be healthy for us. As ruminants, cattle are biologically equipped to eat grasses because they have a second stomach, or "rumen" where grasses can be digested. Cattle are not suited for a corn diet, which has too much starch and not enough roughage for rumination to take place. When a cow is put on a corn diet to fatten it for slaughter, gas can become trapped in the rumen, inflating it to the point that it can press on the lungs and suffocate the animal. Unlike a diet of grasses, a corn diet also makes the cow's stomach acidic, which can lead to ulcers that eat into the wall of the rumen, releasing bacteria into the bloodstream. Cattle must then be fed antibiotics to keep them healthy. Just as a corn diet is not the healthy choice for cattle, corn-fed beef may not be the healthiest choice for our dinner table. Although Americans have grown to prefer the taste and texture of corn-fed beef, the meat itself has more saturated fat and less of the healthy omega-3 fatty acids found in grass-fed cattle. In addition, the more acidic cattle stomachs may have lead to the strains of *E.coli* that can tolerate human stomach acids, causing serious illness or even death. Furthermore, some scientists believe the increased use of antibiotics in cattle is contributing to the evolution of antibiotic-resistant superbugs. Even though fattening cattle on corn may be a less expensive and more efficient way to bring beef to our dinner tables, we should think twice before sinking our teeth into corn-fed beef burgers.

1. Underline the topic sentence. According to this sentence, the writer is trying to convince you of what?

2. What evidence does the writer give to show that a corn diet is not healthy for cattle?

3. What evidence does the writer give to show that eating corn-fed cattle may not be healthy for people?

47

4. What opposing arguments does this writer address? What opposing arguments should be addressed before you would accept this writer's position?

5. Give three examples of key words the writer repeats.

   _____   _____   _____

6. Give four examples of transitional words and phrases the writer uses.

   _____   _____   _____   _____

7. Explain how the writer incorporates each of the following modes into this paragraph:

   definition

   comparison/contrast

   cause and effect

8. What would be an effective title for this paragraph?

Building a Persuasion Paragraph

Write a paragraph in which you persuade your readers to eat or not to eat some type of food or food product. Perhaps you have concerns about food additives like aspartame or high fructose corn syrup, and you want to warn people to avoid those products. Or you may think that a local bakery has the best cream-filled donuts in town, and you want to share the news, so others can enjoy them. Or you might try to convince your readers that higher-priced organic food is worth the cost. Your audience for this paragraph is readers who may not initially want to follow your advice.

Step #1—Freewriting and Brainstorming First, freewrite for about ten minutes, putting down all the reasons you think people should or should not eat certain foods or food products. Just let the ideas flow. Then, once you have decided upon what your subject will be, engage in more focused brainstorming by using the following prompts:

Why people should or should not eat this:	Why might people disagree with me?	What is my response to their disagreement?

49

Step #2—Organizing Compose a topic sentence and a scratch outline to help organize the points you will use in this paragraph. Your topic sentence should clearly state the stand you are taking on your subject. You might consider organizing your supporting reasons for this stand in emphatic order, so that the paragraph builds up to your strongest reason. Also, consider where in the paragraph you might include your rebuttal—that is how you will address potential objections to your reasons.

TS: _____

_____

First Reason: _____

_____

Second Reason: _____

_____

Third Reason: _____

_____

Fourth Reason:_____

_____

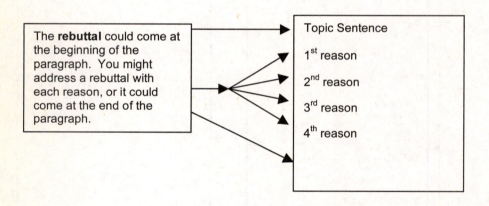

Step #3—Drafting Write a first draft of this paragraph.

Step #4—Analyze the Draft for Revision and Revise

1. According to your topic sentence, what stand are you taking on the consumption of this food or food product? _____

   _____

2. Do all of your sentences stay focused on this subject and support its point? Place a check by any sentences that seem to stray off track.

3. Give two examples of key words you repeat in this paragraph.

   _____   _____

4. Why have you chosen to present your reasons in this particular order?

5. Give three examples of transitions you use in this paragraph.

   _____   _____   _____

6. What examples and details have you chosen to make your points more convincing for the reader?

   _____

   _____

   _____

7. How have you chosen to present your rebuttals? Why did you chose this way to include them?

8. What part of this paragraph do you think the reader will find the most convincing?

9. Which reasons might your reader find not so convincing? What can you do to strengthen them?

10. Based on your responses to these questions, what are the main revisions you plan to make to your draft?

Step #5—Edit Revised Draft

*For more practice with **persuasion (or argument)**, go to www.mywritinglab.com... MyWritingLab...**where better practice makes better writers!***

ANSWER KEY

Identifying Topic Sentence Errors Key

Identify each of the following as a title (T), an announcement (A), too broad (B), a supporting detail (SD) or a topic sentence (TS).

A	I want to discuss the perfume business.
TS	Celebrities are finding the perfume industry to be a money-making venture.
T	A smelly business.
SD	At $215,000 per bottle, Imperial Majesty is the world's most expensive perfume.
B	Perfume-making has undergone many changes since its beginnings in ancient Egypt.

TS	A lack of Vitamin D can cause serious health problems.
SD	Doctors estimate that up to 40% of the U.S. population is Vitamin D deficient.
A	This paragraph will explain how you can get enough Vitamin D through diet and exposure to sunlight.
T	Avoiding D deficiency.
B	Many vitamins are necessary for optimum health, and we can get these vitamins from a variety of sources.

TS	A soccer player can take several precautions to reduce the risk of injury.
SD	Pele, one of soccer's most famous players, retired more than 25 years ago.
A	I will explain how soccer has changed from a village free-for-all in medieval England to the game it is today.
B	Compared to other sports, soccer is much more exciting and interesting.
T	Soccer: an exciting alternative to baseball.

SD	AKC dog events draw nearly two million entries annually.
TS	Dog show judges look for specific "standards" in a particular breed.
T	The road to Best in Show.
A	This paragraph will describe how a dog can become a champion show dog.
B	Throughout history human beings and dogs have had many relationships.

T	Waking up to coffee
A	In this paragraph I will explain how a pope made coffee an acceptable drink for Europeans.
SD	Seven million metric tons of coffee beans are harvested every year.
B	The growing, processing, shipping and marketing of coffee beans is an interesting process.
TS	Pope Clement VIII was able to make coffee a respectable drink for Europeans.

TS	President James Buchanan did little to prevent the Civil War.
T	James Buchanan the bachelor President
B	U.S. Presidents have dealt with many conflicts and handled them in different ways.
SD	Buchanan was so disliked that his portrait was taken down from the Capitol rotunda to prevent it from being vandalized.
A	This paragraph tells about how little President Buchanan did to prevent the war between the states.

Composing Topic Sentences Key

For each of the following sets of details, write the topic sentence which they support. Remember that a topic sentence tells the limited subject and the controlling idea of a paragraph.

TS: A vitamin D deficiency can cause a number of physical problems.
a. Vitamin D deficiency can cause muscle weakness and pain often misdiagnosed as fibromyalgia.
b. Without sufficient levels of vitamin D, the body cannot absorb calcium, which can lead to osteoporosis.
c. A deficiency in Vitamin D can impair the body's ability to produce insulin.
d. Rickets, a bone-wasting disease, is the result of severe vitamin D deficiency.

TS: You can take several steps to write an effective classified ad.
a. Use art, font and layout to attract the eyes of newspaper browsers to your ad.
b. Organize the ad clearly and logically, moving the reader from the headline to the description to the price to the seller contact information.
c. Include specifics about your item such as the brand or model.
d. Urge prospective buyers to act quickly, so they call you first.

TS: Adah Isaacs Menken defied the conventions of her time.
a. In the 1860s, actress Adah Isaacs Menken shocked theater critics by appearing on stage wearing a flesh-colored body stocking and riding a horse.
b. Menken cut her hair short and smoked cigarettes in public during a time when respectable women did neither.
c. Menken refused to perform on stage during Jewish holy days even at the height of her career.
d. Menken married four men in seven years during a time when even one divorce could cause a scandal.

TS: Getting a tattoo involves some health risks.
a. Using tattooing equipment that has not been properly sterilized could lead to the transmission of Hepatitis B, syphilis, and even HIV.
b. Tattoo ink is not regulated, and some people have experienced severe allergic reactions to it.
c. The metallic pigment in some tattoos has caused people to experience pain and burning when they have MRIs.
d. Infections can occur in new tattoos if appropriate aftercare is not followed.

TS: There are some distinct styles of mustaches.
a. Named after the artist Salvador Dali, the Dali mustache is long and thin, curving upwards at the sides.
b. With the Fu Manchu mustache, whiskers along the upper lip are grown very long and allowed to droop down each side of the mouth to the jaw.
c. The Toothbrush mustache, thick and only about an inch wide, was made famous by Adolph Hitler and later Charlie Chaplin.
d. The Handlebar mustache is bushy and grown long enough to curl the ends upwards with styling wax.

TS: Dogs have been used quite successfully in advertising.
a. Spuds Mackenzie, the white bull terrier mascot of Anheuser-Busch Beer, was so popular that an entire line of merchandise was designed around him.
b. Nipper, the fox terrier, has been the longtime symbol of the RCA company.
c. Taco Bell used a Spanish-speaking Chihuahua to sell tacos as well as millions of plush toy replicas of the popular dog.
d. Even The National Crime Prevention Council chose a dog, McGruff, to promote its campaign of crime prevention.

Paragraph Unity Key

Circle the letters of the supporting details that do not support the following topic sentences. (Answers in bold.)

1. TS: Abraham Lincoln's young son Tad could be a terror during the years he spent in the White House.

   a. Once when Lincoln was playing chess with a judge, Tad kicked the chess board, scattering pieces across the floor. Lincoln calmly took Tad's hand and went off to dinner with him.
   b. He broke a large mirror with his ball and ruined a marble table top by running his ink-covered fingers over the top of it.
   c. **Tad begged his father to spare the life of their Thanksgiving turkey and turned it into a pet, leading it around the White House grounds on a string.**
   d. Tad took tubes of paint from an artist who had come to paint Lincoln's portrait and smeared the paint all over the walls while his father looked on smiling.
   e. Tad once drove a team of goats through the East Room of the White House.
   f. **Tad loved money, but he could not understand the difference between the size of a coin and its value. He preferred larger coins over small gold coins that were more valuable.**

2. TS: Color can have an impact on both our mental and physical states.

   a. Perhaps because blue food is so rare, the color blue can cause people to lose their appetites.
   b. Red, however, is a popular food color, and restaurants often use a red color scheme because it stimulates people's appetites.
   c. **In China, red symbolizes luck, so it is used in wedding ceremonies.**
   d. Green is a calming color, which might be why many hospitals use green color schemes, and even surgeons wear green scrubs when operating.
   e. **White is a popular color in fashion because it is neutral and can be worn with anything.**
   f. Pink has a calming, almost tranquilizing effect, so some sports teams have painted the opposing team's locker room pink.

4. TS: Polar bears are particularly suited for life in the cold arctic regions.

   a. **Because ice sheets are melting due to global warming, polar bears are not able to travel as far in their search for food.**
   b. The polar bear's white coat makes it almost invisible as its stalks its prey.
   c. **A single polar bear needs to eat between 50 and 75 seals per year to survive.**
   d. Polar bears have black skin, which absorbs heat, and beneath their skin a layer of blubber keeps the bears well-insulated against the bitter cold.
   e. Soft bumps on the pads of their feet give polar bears the traction they need on slick ice.
   f. Polar bears have two layers of fur: an outer coat of long fur sticks together when wet to form a waterproof barrier, keeping the thick undercoat of fur dry.

4. TS: Wild animals can use tools in clever and innovative ways.

    a. Jane Goodall observed chimpanzees pick and trim long blades of grass, which they then poked into termite mounds to retrieve the tasty insects.
    b. Jane Goodall is considered the world's expert on chimpanzee behavior.
    c. Scientists have seen young animals learn to use tools by watching adults.
    d. Because the tasty ostrich egg has a shell too tough for them to peck open, Egyptian vultures have learned to throw rocks at the egg to crack it open.
    e. Green herons will drop a small object on the surface of water as "bait" and then snatch the fish that rises to the surface.
    f. Orangutans braid vines together to make a stronger rope.

5. TS: Wearing the number 13 has not been lucky for professional athletes.

    a. Pitcher Billy Wagner of the Houston Astros was hit on the side of the head by a line drive and later missed most of a season because of ligament surgery.
    b. Mats Sundin, captain of the Toronto Maple Leafs hockey team, was hit in the face by a puck, and needed fifteen stitches to close the gash between his eyes and forehead.
    c. Wilt Chamberlain is the only basketball player to have scored 100 points in a game and was named to 13 All-Star teams.
    d. Wearing the number 13 during the 1999 baseball season, pitcher Jeff Fassero compiled the worst single season ERA since 1937.
    e. Quarterback Dan Marino entered the Hall of Fame holding all-time records in passing touchdowns and passing yards.
    f. In addition to wearing the unlucky number, Brooklyn Dodger Pitcher Ralph Branca posed with a black cat before the 1951 play-offs where he would become famous for throwing the pitch that led to Bobby Thomson's famous home-run, "a shot heard around the world."

6. In 1905, Diamond Jim Brady, who had earned millions selling railroad equipment, gave an unforgettable party to honor his racehorse, Gold Heels.

    a. For seventeen hours, fifty guests consumed over $40,000 in food
    b. Another New York millionaire gave a dinner honoring his dog, which wore a $15,000 collar to the bash.
    c. Guests drank more than 500 bottles of champagne with their food.
    d. Although he was a voracious eater, Diamond Jim did not drink alcohol.
    e. For "party favors," ladies received diamond brooches, and men received diamond-studded watches.
    f. The entire affair, held at the Hoffman House in New York City, cost more than $100,000.

Levels of Development Key

Part I. Rank the statements in the following sets according to their level of generalization with #1 being the most general and #3 being the least general.

3   a. Tony the Tiger has been roaring about the goodness of Kellogg's Sugar Frosted Flakes since 1952.

1   b. Advertisers often use animals to promote their products.

2   c. Cereal companies have had success using animated animals to promote breakfast cereals.

1   a. Caves provide three different types of habitats.

3   b. Bacteria and tiny multi-celled animals visible only through a microscope are all that can survive in the freezing ice caves of Greenland.

2   c. Glacial ice caves are perhaps the most challenging cave habitat.

3   a. When Arachne bragged that she was the greatest weaver, the goddess Athena turned her into a spider.

2   b. The Greek myths frequently warned people of the dangers of excessive pride.

1   c. Greek mythology explores a full range of interactions between gods and human beings.

2   a. Tidal energy can be used where there are large increases in tide.

3   b. A plant in France currently uses tidal energy to power more than 240,000 homes.

1   c. As the world looks for alternative sources of fuel, the ocean may be a boundless source of energy.

1   a. Wrestling can be more enjoyable and entertaining to watch if you understand how a match is scored.

2   b. If a wrestler cannot win his match by pinning his opponent, he must try to earn the most points in the match.

3   c. A wrestler can score five points by throwing his opponent in a high sweeping arc from a standing position to his back on the floor.

Part II. Each of the following sets should begin with the most general statement and end with the most specific statement. Add the missing level of development to each set.

1.   a. No matter what season of the year it is, the children in my neighborhood enjoy playing outside.
        b. Even in the winter the children find lots to do outside.
        c. Despite the cold, they build snow forts and swoop down hills on their sleds.

2.   **a. Joe's biggest priority in his life is his Mustang.**
        b. Joe even puts caring for his car over his relationships.
        c. He broke up with one girlfriend because going to visit her was putting too many miles on his precious Mustang.

56

3.   a. College teachers hear a full range of excuses from students who miss class.
b. Sometimes the weather provides the perfect excuse.
c. "My locks were frozen, and I couldn't open my car" or "My engine overheated, and my car broke down" are typical weather-related excuses.

4.   a. Dieting can be especially difficult on special occasions.
b. Family celebrations, like birthday parties, always include special foods.
c. Once the candles are blown out, I can't resist helping myself to a heaping plate of cake and ice cream.

5.   a. A date doesn't have to be an expensive night on the town.
b. A local park can be the setting for an inexpensive but enjoyable date.
c. Enjoying a picnic lunch followed by a long walk can be a pleasant and romantic way to spend an afternoon.

6.   a. Eric likes to use his appearance to shock people.
b. Tattoos have become his latest means to draw attention to himself.
c. Brightly colored "sleeves" fill both of his arms, and a green snake coils around his neck.

Answers may vary. These are samples.

Developing a Paragraph with Reasons and Examples Key

Are you or is someone you know part of the Millennial Generation—those Americans born between 1980 and 2000? Complete the following outline to write a paragraph about the Millennials. First, determine which of the reasons listed below support the paragraph's main points and add them to the outline. Then use your personal knowledge of this generation to fill in specific supporting examples. Once the outline is complete, use it to write a paragraph about the Millennials, being sure to add transitions where they are appropriate.
.

TS: The Millennials—those Americans born between 1980 and 2000—have traits that make them a promising generation.

    (First Main Idea) The Millennials are a confident generation.

        (Reason) During the 1990s national attention to children was the highest it had been since the Baby Boomers were kids, and Millennials enjoyed the attention of involved, protective parents who sought to raise their children's self-esteem.

        (Reason) Since they were toddlers, the Millennials have been told through their television shows that they are smart and special.

        (Example) will vary

    (Second Main Idea) The Millennials are patriotic.

        (Reason) September 11, 2001 was a defining moment for the Millennials, and they were a part of the surge in nationalism and patriotism that followed.

        (Reason) More Millennials are showing interest in politics and participation in political elections.

        (Example) will vary

    (Third Main Idea) Growing up in a multi-cultural world, the Millennials are inclusive.

        (Reason) Those growing up in the 90s and 00s have had more interaction with other ethnic groups and races than previous generations.

        (Reason) The Millennials are used to working in teams and have grown up with the notion that no one should be left behind.

        (Example) will vary

In the workplace, Millennials tend to communicate more through technology than face-to-face.

A survey in 2001 showed that parents were most often named when Millennials were asked whom they most admired.

Analyzing Coherence in a Paragraph Key

Read the following paragraph carefully, noting the various ways the writer achieves coherence. Answer the questions that follow.

Space travel has evolved dramatically since the early '60s when John Glenn orbited the earth in a small Mercury capsule. In addition to improving the size, comfort and technological sophistication of the space vehicles, NASA has made eating in space a more enjoyable and tasty experience for astronauts. The first astronauts who tried to eat in the low gravity of a space vehicle squeezed their meals from tubes or sucked them up through straws. For chewing, there were cubes of dehydrated foods, moisturized and reconstituted by the astronaut's own saliva. Later, the Apollo astronauts, who journeyed to the moon, were the first to enjoy meals they could eat with a spoon. (They) injected water into a plastic container filled with their dehydrated meal and once wet, the food would stick to spoons. Apollo astronauts also ate food such as beef sandwiches and chocolate pudding kept moist in aluminum pouches called wetpacks. Beginning in the 1980s, astronauts aboard space shuttles could enjoy a wide variety of soups, casseroles, meats, fresh fruits and vegetables prepared in a galley equipped with a water dispenser for rehydrating foods and a convection oven for heating meals. In 2006, even this diverse menu was "kicked up a notch" by Chef Emeril Lagasse. (He) designed a space menu for the Discovery astronauts that included jambalaya and bread pudding. NASA has plans for future space travelers to dine on fresh lettuce, spinach, rice and peanuts grown in special hydroponic systems aboard space vehicles bound for distant planets.

1. Coherence, the way a writer "connects" ideas in a paragraph, begins with a clear organizational strategy. Which of the following strategies does the writer of the space food paragraph use?

   X   chronological   ____ spatial   ___emphatic

2. What helps you determine that this is the organization strategy?

   The use of dates—'60s, 1980s and 2006—and the transitional word *later* indicate time as the organizing principle.

3. Give three examples of transitional words and phrases the writer uses.
   <u>In addition</u>   <u>The first</u>   <u>Later</u>   <u>Beginning in the 1980s</u>   <u>In 2006</u>

4. A writer may also use pronouns to achieve coherence by having a pronoun refer back to an antecedent in a previous sentence. Find the two pronouns in this paragraph that refer to antecedents in the preceding sentence. Circle the pronoun and draw a line to the antecedent.

59

5. A writer also achieves coherence by repeating key words—nouns, adjectives and verbs. Give four examples of key words that are repeated in this paragraph.
<u>astronauts</u> <u>eat</u> <u>meals</u> <u>space</u> <u>NASA</u> <u>food</u>

6. Sometimes, instead of repeating a word, a writer may use a synonym. What synonym for the key word *eat* does the writer use?
<u>dine</u>

What synonym for *astronauts* does the writer use?
<u>space travelers</u>

Paragraph Analysis Key

Read the following paragraph carefully and then match the instructor's comments to the sections of the paragraphs to which they refer.

The Most Famous Yell In The World

Perhaps the most famous yell in the world is the distinctive Tarzan yell used by Johnny Weissmuller in the Tarzan movies of the 1930s. Although there are stories about how the studio technicians created the yell by mixing a variety of sounds, Weissmuller claimed the yell was his own variation of the yodeling he had done as a young boy in Romania. Once he perfected the yell, technicians recorded it and for nearly fifty years used it in Tarzan movies. The yell was so famous and inspiring that during World War II it was broadcasted to the soldiers on the battlefront. Perhaps because he was so identified with his Tarzan yell, Weissmuller asked that a recording of the yell be played at his funeral. Weissmuller even said the yell once saved his life in 1959 when he was on his way to a golf tournament in Havana, Cuba. Castro's rebel forces had surrounded his car when Weissmuller cut loose with his famous yell. The soldiers immediately recognized the famous Tarzan, they escorted him safely to the tournament. In his later years, when Weissmuller attempted the yell, he would be hoarse for days. Long after Weissmuller's death, variations of the yell continue to show up. The comedian Carol Burnett, who had learned the yell as a child, frequently used it in her tv comedy show, which ran from 1967-'78. A variation of the yell was used in the movie *George of the Jungle*. The yell has also been heard in the James Bond film *Octopussy* and George Lucas's *Star Wars: Revenge of the Sith*.

Instructor's comments:

- #3: Sentence error--capitalization
- #2: This topic sentence shows a clear subject and controlling idea
- #5: Good use of pronoun reference to achieve coherence
- #1: Coherence—Are you using chronological order consistently?
- #9: Sentence error—comma splice
- #6: Unity—Does this support the idea that the yell is distinctive and well-known?
- #4: Good transition
- #8: Ends a bit abruptly—conclusion?

1. Coherence—Are you using chronological order consistently?

2. This topic sentence shows a clear subject and controlling idea.

3. Sentence error—capitalization

4. Good transition

5. Good use of pronoun reference to achieve coherence

6. Unity—Does this support the idea that the yell is distinctive and well-known?

7. Nice repetition of key words

8. Ends a bit abruptly—conclusion?

9. Sentence error—comma splice

Analyzing a Description Paragraph Key

The following paragraph describes the ruins of Khara Khoto—or the Black City—which lies in the desolate Gobi desert of China. Read it carefully and answer the questions that follow.

In 1908, Colonel Pyotr Kuzmich Koslov, leader of a Russian Expedition to Mongolia, came upon the ruins of the lost city of Khara Khoto in the middle of the Gobi desert between China and Mongolia. The desolate, some say haunted, ruins of this desert city stand in silent testimony to the fragility of human settlement. Once a thriving Mongol city visited by Marco Polo, Khara Khoto had fertile fields where herds of cattle and camel grazed, and a life-giving river flowed right up to its massive walls. It was this river, according to local legends, that armies of the invading Ming Dynasty diverted away from the city in 1372. When the city's defenders grew weak by starvation and thirst under the relentless desert sun, the invaders breached the walls, sacked the city and massacred its inhabitants. Today, the Chinese say, the ghosts left by this merciless slaughter haunt the sand-filled streets and crumbling mud buildings. Tourists may come to gaze upon the twelve-foot thick outer city walls, the thirty-foot tall ramparts and the towers that still stand against the cloudless blue sky, but rarely does anyone venture into the dead city, even in the daylight. Even stories of a hoard of gold hidden by the doomed Mongol king do not entice adventure seekers. At night, only the wind stirs the sand that covers the shattered pottery, the bleached bones within the city walls.

1. Which adjectives best describe this desert city before the Ming invaders arrived?
Thriving, fertile, life-giving

2. Which words in this section of the paragraph work together to create a unified expression of the city as it is today?
Ghost, sand-filled, crumbling, cloudless, dead city, doomed, shattered, bleached bones

3. This paragraph begins with the discovery of the city's ruins. Was this beginning an effective way to get the readers' attention? Why or why not?

    Answers will vary.

4. The writer uses description to make a point about life, about the human condition. What is this point?

    Existence is fragile.

5. Explain how the writer incorporates the following rhetorical modes into this description paragraph: comparison/contrast and narration.

    The paragraph shows the city before and after the invasion (compare/contrast). The paragraph tells the story of the invasion (narrative).

6. Some might argue that this paragraph ends abruptly. Write a sentence that clearly concludes the paragraph—perhaps by referring back to one of the opening sentences.

Answers will vary.

7. Circle the letter of the correct form for this paragraph's title.

a) Ghosts in the Desert
b. GHOSTS IN THE DESERT
c. Ghosts In The Desert
d. Ghosts in the desert

Analyzing a Narrative Paragraph Key

A narrative tells a story that often offers some insights into people we will never meet and experiences we will never have ourselves. Such narratives may satisfy our curiosity or help us better understand why people behave the way they do.

The following narrative is about Robert Pershing Wadlow, better known as the Alton Giant. At the time of his death in 1940, Wadlow was 8'11.1" tall, making him the tallest person in history according to the Guinness Book of World Records. A quiet, somewhat shy man, Wadlow spent his short life in Alton, Illinois, when he wasn't traveling with his father promoting a shoe company that provided him with his own size 37 AAA shoes. Read the paragraph carefully and answer the questions that follow.

When Robert Wadlow was twenty-years-old, he and his father set out on a countrywide promotional tour for a shoe company. <u>After his father removed the front passenger seat of the family car,</u> Robert climbed in the back seat, stretching out his long legs, and the two of them set off on a 300,000 mile tour to over 800 towns in 41 states. <u>During one stop</u> in Hot Springs, Arkansas, Robert and Mr. Wadlow decided to go with some friends to see a night club show. A friend called ahead for reservations and was told that men attending the show were required to wear a coat or jacket. Knowing that Robert had not packed a coat or jacket for a trip to Arkansas in sweltering summer heat, the friend said that the group had a young man who did not have proper attire. He was reassured that the club provided "loaners" for such patrons. "<u>But</u> this is a 'big' boy," the friend tried to explain. <u>Again</u> he was reassured that the club had big coats and jackets to loan to patrons. <u>When Robert arrived at the club</u> with his father and friends, the host could only stare at the 8'11" gentle giant who weighed over four hundred pounds and stammer, "He *is* a big boy, isn't he." Robert was able to see the show without a coat or jacket.

1. This paragraph does not have an explicit topic sentence. How does the writer still keep the paragraph unified? What point does the paragraph make about rules?

   The writer focuses on one anecdote and does not try to cover too much about the entire trip Robert and his father went on. Sometimes there are very good reasons to make exceptions to a rule.

2. What does this incident help you understand about Robert Wadlow? What do you learn about the people who met Robert?

   It seems like people from Robert's father to the friends and even the night club host tried to accommodate Robert so he could enjoy everyday experiences despite his enormous size. One gets the sense that Robert was good natured about the reactions he undoubtedly got from people who saw him for the first time.

3. Why doesn't this paragraph go on to discuss more of the experiences Robert and his father had on the tour?

   A paragraph cannot cover so much material without losing unity and coherence. The entire trip might be better described in an essay.

4. A narrative follows a chronological order. Underline the transitional words and phrases the writer uses to connect the parts of the story.

5. What details make the experience described here more vivid for the readers?

   Answers will vary.

6. What would be a good title for this paragraph? Be sure to capitalize the title properly.

   Answers will vary.

Analyzing an Illustration Paragraph Key

An illustration paragraph uses examples to "show" the writer's point about the subject. The following paragraph shows what a compulsive gambler John Warne Gates, a turn-of-the-century millionaire businessman, was. Read it carefully and answer the questions that follow.

1. What does the writer do to generate the readers' interest in the subject?

The reader may wonder how one can be both a successful businessman and a gambler. Also, the nickname generates interest—what did he bet a million on?

John Warne Gates was an astute businessman, a speculator who competed with financial giants like J.P. Morgan and Andrew Carnegie. However, Gates is best remembered for his compulsive, no-holds-barred gambling that earned him the nickname "Bet-A-Million." Gates's obsession with gambling began when he was a schoolboy in Turner's Junction, where he played poker with railroad workers. As an adult, Gates might lose a million dollars in poker marathons that lasted several days, but he always won more than he lost. And he was a fearless gambler, earning his nickname by trying to place a million dollar bet on a horse at the Saratoga race track. If horses, cards, dice and roulette were not around, Gates would bet on anything available. Once a Kansas City sports writer, representing a syndicate, placed a $40,000 wager on any game Gates chose. Gates flipped a gold piece and asked the writer to call "Heads or tails." The writer then became known as the man who lost $40,000 in ten seconds to Bet-A-Million Gates. Wealthy playboy John Drake also lost a small fortune to Gates in an impulsive wager. Each man dunked a piece of bread in his coffee and then set the bread on the table to attract flies. The one whose bread attracted the most flies would win $1,000 per fly. Gates won a small fortune probably because he had sweetened his coffee with six cubes of sugar before dunking his bread. It was the same shrewd gambling spirit that later led Gates to make millions in Texas oil speculations before his death in 1911.

2. What two coherence devices are combined here?

The writer uses a transition—and. Also, the pronoun he refers to Gates in the previous sentence.

3. What are some of the specific details the writer includes here to make the examples more vivid and interesting?

There are specific dollar amounts-- $40,000 and $1,000. Gates flipped a "gold piece." Telling about so much money being lost in only thirty seconds emphasizes the impulsiveness and riskiness of the gambles. Saying John Drake was a playboy makes his losing to Gates's cunning more humorous.

4. How does this key word connect the conclusion to the introduction and bring the paragraph full circle?

Gates's business success and gambling success were both types of "speculations" that took a willingness to act fearlessly.

5. The author uses examples to show that Gates was a gambler. How do these examples also show that Gates was "fearless" and "compulsive"?

Answers will vary.

6. What would be a good title for this paragraph? Be sure to capitalize the title properly.

Answers will vary.

Analyzing a Process Paragraph Key

The following paragraph describes foot binding, a custom that began in China nearly a thousand years ago and continued up until the early 1900s. Read it carefully and answer the questions that follow.

For several centuries, women in China had their feet bound in order to achieve their culture's ideal of beauty. **This process of binding the feet to stunt their growth was both painful and dangerous.** When a Chinese girl was four to six years old, her mother would begin the foot binding process during the winter months when the cold could help numb the pain. After having her feet soaked in warm water or animal blood, the young girl would have her toe nails cut very short to prevent them from growing into the flesh of her foot. Then the mother would massage her daughter's feet before breaking the four smallest toes on each foot. Even greater pain followed when the mother would wrap about ten feet of silk or cotton bandages around the girl's toes and pull them tightly, bending the ball of the foot to the heel. Every two days the bandages would be removed, rebound and pulled even tighter. Following two years of this process, a girl's feet were only three to four inches long. During this time, pain was constant, serious infection was common and even death from infection was a possibility.

1. Underline the topic sentence of this paragraph. According to this topic sentence, the subject or topic of the paragraph is <u>Chinese foot binding</u>, and the point the writer wants to make is <u>the process is painful and dangerous</u>.

2. Which organizational pattern does this paragraph follow?

   <u>X</u> chronological   ___ spatial   ___ emphatic

3. Give two examples of key words that are repeated in this paragraph.

   <u>pain feet/foot girl mother China/Chinese</u>

4. Give three examples of transitional words or phrases used in this paragraph.

   <u>After   Then   Even greater pain followed   Following two years of this process   During this time</u>

5. Give two examples of specific details the writer uses in this paragraph.   (Answers will vary)

6. Which of the following would be the best title for this paragraph?
   a. A Process Paragraph
   b. Foot Binding in China
   c. A Painful Practice
   d. The Painful Price for Beauty

67

Analyzing a Comparison/Contrast Paragraph Key

The following paragraph compares the historical Jesse James to the Jesse James often depicted in movies and books. Read the paragraph carefully and then label the parts as indicated.

Topic sentence →

Transition

Repeated key word

Transition

Transition

Synonym

Specific detail

Despite the romanticized story of his life in movies and books, the outlaw Jesse James was not a heroic, western Robin Hood. One myth about Jesse James is that he and his brother, Frank, robbed the railroads because the railroad companies forced the brothers off their land. In reality, the railroads were already established in the area when the James brothers began holding up and robbing trains. It's more likely the James brothers began robbing trains because banks had increased security and began using time lock vaults. Nor was Jesse James forced into crime because as a Southern sympathizer, he could not find work after the Civil War. Although times were hard following the war, James had uncles in Kansas City who were successful businessmen willing to help out family members by giving them jobs. Jesse James chose robbery as a way of life; he was not forced into it. An even bigger myth is that James robbed from the rich and gave to the poor. The local banks James robbed were not federally insured, so the townspeople and farmers lost money. And when the James gang robbed a train or stage coach, they took money from anyone who happened to be aboard. In the course of fifteen years, the James gang committed at least twenty-six hold-ups, made off with more than $200,000 and killed at least seventeen men, some unarmed and some innocent by-standers. The only ones who benefited financially from these crimes were the robbers' families. Far from being a Robin Hood, Jesse James stole from anyone and kept the money for himself.

1. Identify the following:

   the topic sentence
   four transitions
   a repeated key word
   specific details
   a synonym for *robberies*

2. Besides showing that the real Jesse James is not the same man depicted in movies and books, what larger point or lesson might be seen in this paragraph?

   Sometimes the general perception of a person may not be based on facts, but on a reputation. Criminals are seldom Robin Hoods. Typical criminals are out for person gain.

68

3. This comparison/contrast paragraph follows a point-by-point pattern. Rewrite it using a block pattern of organization.

Example:

Despite the romanticized story of his life in movies and books, the outlaw Jesse James was not a heroic, western Robin Hood. According to legends, Jesse James and his brother, Frank, robbed the railroads because the railroad companies forced the brothers off their land. Not only was he unable to farm, but Jesse James was forced into crime because as a Southern sympathizer, he could not find work after the Civil War. So Jesse James, it was said, became a bank and train robber as the only way he could support his family. But he did not forget others who were living in hard times. He didn't rob from the poor and gave some of the money he stole from the rich to the poor. While these stories might make great books and movies, Jesse James's life of crime was much different. In reality, the railroads were already established in the area when the James brothers began holding up and robbing trains. It's more likely the James brothers began robbing trains because banks had increased security and began using time lock vaults. And although times were hard following the war, James had uncles in Kansas City who were successful businessmen willing to help out family members by giving them jobs. Jesse James chose robbery as a way of life; he was not forced into it. The local banks James robbed were not federally insured, so the townspeople and farmers, rich and poor, lost money. When the James gang robbed a train or stage coach, they took money from anyone who happened to be aboard. In the course of fifteen years, the James gang committed at least twenty-six hold-ups, made off with more than $200,000 and killed at least seventeen men, some unarmed and some innocent by-standers. The only ones who benefitted financially from these crimes were the robbers' families. Far from being a Robin Hood, Jesse James stole from anyone and kept the money for himself.

4. Which title best fits this paragraph?

    a. Looking at Truth and Legend
    b. A Famous Robber
    c. Jesse James: Hero or Criminal?
    d. Jesse James

69

Analyzing a Cause and Effect Paragraph Key

The following paragraph tells some of the reasons (causes) people are fired from their jobs. Read the paragraph carefully and answer the questions that follow.

<u>Getting fired often involves ignoring some basic expectations</u>. Employers expect their employees to know how to do the work they were hired to do. Those employees who overstated their experience or qualifications during a job interview may find themselves fired if they cannot quickly learn their jobs. Similarly, frustrated employers will fire those who work too slowly and make frequent errors. Employers also expect employees to get along with their colleagues. While some people have more social skills than others, all employees can show respect towards their co-workers. Most employers will not tolerate employees who spread malicious gossip, blame colleagues for problems, and behave rudely toward others. Perhaps the most important expectation employers have is honesty. Employees who falsify time sheets, expense reports and project reports nearly always face termination when they are caught. Stealing company materials and equipment is grounds for dismissal as well as using company resources and time for non-company business. Employers expect employees to be qualified, personable and honest. Someone not meeting these expectations will soon hear the dreaded words, "You're fired!"

1. Underline the topic sentence. According to this topic sentence, the effect is
   <u>getting fired</u> , which is caused by <u>not meeting expectations</u> .

2. Which organizational pattern does this paragraph follow?
   __ chronological   __ spatial   _X_ emphatic

3. Give three examples of key words that are repeated.
   <u>employers</u>   <u>employees</u>   <u>fire/fired</u>   <u>expectations</u>   <u>honest/honesty</u>

4. What word is a synonym for *colleagues*?
   <u>co-workers</u>

5. Give three examples of transitional words or phrases.
   <u>Similarly</u>   <u>also</u>   <u>Perhaps the most important</u>

6. Circle the letter that shows the correct form of the title of this paragraph.
   a. HOW TO GET FIRED
   b. How To Get Fired
   c. How to Get Fired
   d. How to get Fired

Analyzing a Classification Paragraph Key

Dog shows have grown increasingly popular, and the most recent Best in Show winner of the prestigious Westminster Kennel Club dog show, a beagle named Uno, has become a celebrity, even appearing on talk shows. Before Uno could compete for Best in Show, he had to win Best in Breed by competing against other beagles. He then had to win the Group competition. The following paragraph discusses the various groups of dogs designated by the American Kennel Club (AKC). Read it carefully and answer the questions that follow.

The American Kennel Club (AKC) recognizes over a 150 breeds of dogs, and has classified these dogs into seven groups for competing in dog shows. The first group, called the Sporting Group, consists of dogs bred specifically to help hunters flush and retrieve game. These energetic, even-tempered dogs include such breeds as Labrador retrievers and Irish setters. Also known to be excellent hunting dogs, hounds were given their own group, the Hound Group, in 1930. The breeds in this group range in size from the Irish wolfhound to the beagle and dachshund. Most hounds are known for their superior sense of smell and habit of baying loudly when on the trail of game. Some of the strongest and most intelligent dogs fall into the Working Group. Dogs such as the St. Bernard, the mastiff, the great dane and the Siberian husky were bred to guard property, to pull carts and sleds and to engage in rescue work. Feisty, strong-willed terriers make up the fourth group. Breeds in the Terrier Group were originally bred to hunt and kill vermin though today few owners of Airedales, schnauzers and Scottish terriers send their dogs after rats. Dogs bred to be small, loving companions make up the Toy Group. Understandably, some of the most popular breeds of pets—toy poodles, Chihuahuas, Yorkshire terriers and Pomeranians—make up this group. The sixth group, the Non-Sporting Group, is a mixed bag of breeds, diverse in size, temperament and function. Bulldogs, Dalmatians, standard poodles and Lhasa apsos are among the dogs in this group. The last group consists of dogs bred for their ability to herd other animals. The collie, German shepherd, Welsh corgi and Australian cattle dogs are all members of the Herding Group. In the world of competitive all-breed dog shows, only those dogs that have won in their group can go on to compete to be Best in Show.

1. Most things can be classified, or put into groups, on the basis of different criteria or ruling principles. Upon what does the American Kennel Club base its classification of dogs?

    The classification is based on the traits for which the dogs were bred.

2. When using classification, writers can sometimes fall into the trap of using redundant sentence structures and predictable transitions: "The first category of dogs is the Sporting Group. . . . The second category of dogs is the Hound Group. . . . The third category of dogs is the Working Group. . . . and so on." What does this writer do to keep the sentences varied and the paragraph coherent?

The writer avoids using the same type of transition to introduce each group. Sometimes the writer begins with the name of the group, other times with the group's characteristics, and other times with examples of the breeds that make up the group. Even though the writer discusses the name of the group, its traits, and the breeds that make it up in each category, by varying the way these points are presented, the writer avoids sounding droning and monotonous.

3. Give three examples of key words that the writer repeats.
   Group dog   show   breed

4. Give examples of three transitional words or phrases the writer uses.
   The first group also   The last group

5. Besides examples of the breeds in each group, what other examples does the writer use to clarify the distinctions among the various groups of dogs?

   The writer gives examples of the dogs' traits—even temper, keen sense of smell, herding ability—and examples of the kinds of work the dogs do—hunting, rescue, companionship.

6. How does the concluding sentence relate back to the first sentence in the paragraph?

   Both sentences refer to dog show groups. The last sentence clarifies the place of the Group shows in the quest to win the highest honor—Best in Show.

7. What would be a good title for this paragraph?

   Answers will vary.

Analyzing a Definition Paragraph Key

The following paragraph defines celiac disease, a disorder affecting over two million Americans. Read it carefully and answer the questions that follow.

You may have noticed a section in your grocery store that carries products labeled "gluten-free." While anyone may eat and enjoy gluten-free foods, for people with celiac disease, these foods offer healthy alternatives to many foods most of us take for granted. Can you imagine never being able to eat anything with wheat, barley or rye ingredients? Along with cakes, cookies and other bakery items, you couldn't eat a wide variety of processed food ranging from pasta and potato chips to cold cuts because they contain wheat and wheat by-products. For people with celiac disease, such a restrictive diet is a life-long necessity for good health because their bodies cannot tolerate the protein gluten, which is found in wheat, barley and rye. When people with celiac disease eat gluten, they seriously damage their small intestines, and food cannot be absorbed into the bloodstream, resulting in malnutrition no matter how much food is eaten. In addition to malnutrition, people with untreated celiac disease are at risk for anemia, osteoporosis, seizures and cancer. Even the early symptoms of celiac disease can be painful or unpleasant, including stomach bloating, gas, chronic diarrhea or constipation, joint pain, irritability and fatigue. For the estimated 1 in 133 Americans with celiac disease, only a lifelong gluten-free diet offers the chance for a healthy life.

1. This paragraph defines celiac disease. What else does it define?

   It also defines "gluten" and "gluten-free diet."

2. What does the writer do to generate interest in readers who do not have this disease or who may know nothing about it?

   Even those without this disease may have noticed products labeled "gluten-free" in grocery stores and been curious about them.

3. What specific examples in this paragraph help to clarify the terms being defined or explained?

   The writer lists specific products that may contain wheat—cakes, cookies, pasta, chips—to show why gluten-free products offer variety and a healthy alternative for those with celiac disease. Specific examples of serious side effects—malnutrition, anemia, cancer—and examples of early symptoms—bloating, gas, diarrhea, joint pain—also help to explain the disease.

4. Underline the words and phrases that help the organization or flow of ideas in this paragraph.

5. What other information about celiac disease might have been included in this paragraph to help the readers' understanding of this disease?

Students may want to know how the disease is diagnosed, at what age symptoms typically become noticeable, what research is underway to find a cure.

6. Which of the following titles is properly capitalized?

    a. Eating For Life With Celiac Disease
    b. EATING FOR LIFE WITH CELIAC DISEASE
    c. Eating for Life With Celiac Disease
    d. Eating for Life with Celiac Disease

Analyzing a Persuasion Paragraph Key

A persuasion paragraph offers convincing evidence in order to take a stand on a controversial subject. In this paragraph, the writer looks at what many consumers do not consider: how food is processed before being brought to the grocery store and labeled. Read the following paragraph carefully and answer the questions that follow.

We often hear groceries and restaurants tout their beef products as coming from "corn-fed" cattle. The implication is that this meat is more wholesome and good. <u>However, being corn-fed is not healthy for the cattle, and eating corn-fed cattle may not be healthy for us</u>. As ruminants, cattle are biologically equipped to eat grasses because they have a second stomach, or "rumen" where grasses can be digested. Cattle are not suited for a corn diet, which has too much starch and not enough roughage for rumination to take place. When a cow is put on a corn diet to fatten it for slaughter, gas can become trapped in the rumen, inflating it to the point that it can press on the lungs and suffocate the animal. Unlike a diet of grasses, a corn diet also makes the cow's stomach acidic, which can lead to ulcers that eat into the wall of the rumen, releasing bacteria into the bloodstream. Cattle must then be fed antibiotics to keep them healthy.   Just as a corn diet is not the healthy choice for cattle, corn-fed beef may not be the healthiest choice for our dinner table.   Although Americans have grown to prefer the taste and texture of corn-fed beef, the meat itself has more saturated fat and less of the healthy omega-3 fatty acids found in grass-fed cattle. In addition, the more acidic cattle stomachs may have lead to the strains of *E.coli* that can tolerate human stomach acids, causing serious illness or even death.   Furthermore, some scientists believe the increased use of antibiotics in cattle is contributing to the evolution of antibiotic-resistant superbugs.   Even though fattening cattle on corn may be a less expensive and more efficient way to bring beef to our dinner tables, we should think twice before sinking our teeth into corn-fed beef burgers.

1. Underline the topic sentence. According to this sentence, the writer is trying to convince you of what?

    The practice of fattening cattle on corn before they are slaughtered is not a healthy one.

2. What evidence does the writer give to show that a corn diet is not healthy for cattle?

    The writer explains that the cow is biologically suited for eating grass, and a corn diet causes physiological problems that often require treatment with antibiotics.

3. What evidence does the writer give to show that eating corn-fed cattle may not be healthy for people?

Copyright © 2010 Pearson Education, Inc. Publishing as Longman.

Corn-fed beef may have fewer healthy omega-3 fatty acids than that which comes from grass-fed cattle. The acidic stomachs of corn-fed cattle may have led to more lethal forms of *E.coli*. The use of antibiotics in cattle may also contribute to more antibiotic-resistant superbugs.

4. What opposing arguments does this writer address? What opposing arguments should be addressed before you would accept this writer's position?

   Opponents would point out that corn-fed beef tastes better. Corn-feeding fattens the cattle quickly and economically, keeping beef affordable. Most cattle are slaughtered before they show the negative effects of a corn diet.
   Answers will vary.

5. Give three examples of key words the writer repeats.
   Cattle beef corn healthy

6. Give four examples of transitional words and phrases the writer uses.
   However   In addition   Furthermore   the sentence: Just as a corn diet is not the healthy choice for cattle, corn-fed beef may not be the healthiest choice for our dinner table.

7. Explain how the writer incorporates each of the following modes into this paragraph:
   definition   The writer defines *ruminant* and *rumen.*

   comparison/contrast The writer shows the difference between grass-fed cattle and corn-fed cattle.

   cause and effect   The paragraph discusses the immediate effects of a corn diet on cattle and the possible later effects on people of eating corn-fed beef.

8. What would be an effective title for this paragraph?

   Answers will vary.

Paragraph Workbook Resources

Identifying Topic Sentence Errors—Miscellaneous
Perfume-- http://www.jurgita.com/articles-id2183.html#void http://www.thehistoryof.net/the-history-of-perfume.html
Vitamin D-- http://www.naturalnews.com/z003069.html
Soccer-- http://www.thehistoryof.net
Dog shows-- http://www.westminsterkennelclub.org/dogshows/aboutdogshows.html
Coffee-- http://www.associatedcontent.com/article/574455/clement_viii_the_pope_who_popularized.html
Buchannon-- http://www.picturehistory.com/find/c/352/mcms.html

Composing Topic Sentences—Miscellaneous
Vitamin D-- http://www.naturalnews.com/z003069.html
Ads-- http://www.adn.com/classified/v-tips/index.html
Menken-- http://www.jewishvirtuallibrary.org/jsource/biography/AMenken.html
Tattoos-- http://kidshealth.org/teen/your_body/skin_stuff/safe_tattooing.html
Mustaches-- www.americanmustacheinstitute.org/MustacheHistory.aspx
Animal mascots-- http://www.tvacres.com/advertising_mascots_animals.htm

Paragraph Unity
Tad Lincoln-- http://www.picturehistory.com/find/c/355/mcms.html
Color-- http://www.infoplease.com/spot/colors1.html
        http://iit.bloomu.edu/vthc/Design/psychology.htm
Polar bears-- http://www.knownfacts.info/polar-bear-facts.php
        http://www.itk.ca/environment/wildlife-polar-bear.php
        http://www.athropolis.com/arctic-facts/fact-polar-bear-pred.htm
        http://www.alaskazoo.org/willowcrest/polarbearhome.htm
Animals w/ tools-- http://www.csmonitor.com/2005/0419/p18s02-hfks.html
13--http://www.infoplease.com/spot/superstitions2.html
Diamond Jim-- http://www.trivia-library.com/famous-fabulous-feasts-in-history/index.htm

Levels of Development
Tidal energy--http://www.energyquest.ca.gov/story/chapter14.html
Caves-- http://www.amazingcaves.com/set_learn_ecology.html
Wrestling-- http://www.saskwrestling.com/watching_a_match.htm
Tony the Tiger-- http://www.tvacres.com/advertising_mascots_animals.htm

Developing a Paragraph with Reasons and Examples
Millennials-- http://humanresources.about.com/od/glossarym/g/millenials.htm

Analyzing Coherence
Space food-- http://science.howstuffworks.com/space-food1.htm
Paragraph Analysis
Tarzan Yell-- http://www.erbzine.com/mag14/1482.html
Analyzing a Description Paragraph
Khara Koto-- http://science.nationalgeographic.com/science/earth/surface-of-the-earth/alashan-plateau-article.html
        http://idp.bl.uk/archives/news02/idpnews_02.a4d#2

77

Analyzing a Narrative Paragraph
Robert Wadlow-- www.he.net/~**alton**web/history/wadlow/
Analyzing an Illustration Paragraph
"Bet a Million" Gates-- http://www.dountoothers.org/americaneccentrics.html
Analyzing a Process Paragraph
Footbinding-- http://www.ccds.charlotte.nc.us/History/China/04/hutchins/hutchins.htm
Analyzing a Comparison/Contrast Paragraph
Jesse James-- http://www.legendsofamerica.com/WE-JesseJames7.html

Building a Comparison/Contrast Paragraph
Customs-- http://washington.bizjournals.com/washington/stories/2007/10/29/smallb8.html
Analyzing Cause and Effect Paragraph
Getting fired-- http://www.forbes.com/business/2006/05/03/business-basics-stupid-firing-cx_sr_0504sacked.html
        http://hubpages.com/hub/Fired
Analyzing a Classification paper—
Dog shows-- http://www.westminsterkennelclub.org/dogshows/aboutdogshows.html
        http://www.akc.org/events/conformation/beginners.cfm
        http://www.canismajor.com/dog/conshow.html
Analyzing a Definition Paragraph
Celiac Disease--http://www.digestive.niddk.nih.gov/ddiseases/pubs/celiac/index.htm
Building a Definition Paragraph
Cryptozoology--http://www.pibburns.com/cryptozo.htm
        http://www.unmuseum.org/found.htm
        http://web.ncf.ca/bz050/criticalcz.html
        http://www.cryptomundo.com/cryptozoo-news/be-czist/
        http://www.cryptozoology.com/articles/wic.php
        http://www.lorencoleman.com/cryptozoology_faq.html#field

Analyzing a Persuasive Paragraph
Corn-fed beef—information taken from Michael Pollan's *The Omnivore's Dilemma*